Praise for
A Nation on Trial

(*CHI.*)

"Is Daniel Goldhagen's *Hitler's Willing Executioners* the definitive work on Hitler's Judeocide? The authors of this volume express serious doubt, which I share. To reduce a phenomenon of this scale and complexity to the anti-Semitism which permeated German society as it also permeated many other societies is to be simplistic and to show contempt for the reader. This book rights the balance."

—PIERRE VIDAL-NAQUET,
author of *The Jews: History, Memory, and the Present*

"Highly recommended to the many readers of Goldhagen's controversial book, especially those who were mesmerized by its hypotheses. Fortunately, in an open society all scholarship is subject to public scrutiny, and the advance of historical knowledge cannot do without rigorous criticism of the kind provided in this important and courageous collection."

—VOLKER R. BERGHAHN,
J. P. Birkelund Professor of
European History, Brown University

"Birn's and Finkelstein's essays constitute a sharp rebuttal provoked by the public's and the press's love affair with a book that casually dismisses excellent work done by others; that contains many contradictions; and that upholds dangerous myths regarding the existence of "national characteristics.""

—ISTVÁN DEÁK,
author of *Beyond Nationalism*

A NATION ON TRIAL

A NATION ON TRIAL

The Goldhagen Thesis and Historical Truth

NORMAN G. FINKELSTEIN

AND

RUTH BETTINA BIRN

AN OWL BOOK

HENRY HOLT AND COMPANY

NEW YORK

Henry Holt and Company, Inc.
Publishers since 1866
115 West 18th Street
New York, New York 10011

Henry Holt is an imprint of Henry Holt and Company, Inc.

A shorter version of "Daniel Jonah Goldhagen's 'Crazy' Thesis"
originally appeared in *New Left Review,* July/August 1997.
"Revising the Holocaust" originally appeared in a slightly shorter
version in *The Historical Journal,* 40.1 (1997).

Library of Congress Cataloging-in-Publication Data
Finkelstein, Norman G.
A nation on trial : the Goldhagen thesis and historical truth /
Norman G. Finkelstein and Ruth Bettina Birn.—1st ed.
p.   cm.
Includes bibliographical references.
ISBN 0-8050-5871-0 (alk. paper).—
ISBN 0-8050-5872-9 (pbk. : alk. paper)
1. Goldhagen, Daniel Jonah. Hitler's willing executioners.
2. Holocaust, Jewish (1939–1945)—Causes.   3. Antisemitism—Germany.
4. War criminals—Germany—Psychology.   5. National socialism—Moral
and ethical aspects.   I. Birn, Ruth Bettina, 1952–   .   II. Title.
D804.G4F53   1998   97-42632
940.53'18—dc21   CIP

Henry Holt books are available for special promotions and premiums.
For details contact: Director, Special Markets.

First Owl Books Edition 1998

Designed by Debbie Glasserman

Printed in the United States of America
All first editions are printed on acid-free paper. ∞

1   3   5   7   9   10   8   6   4   2

Acknowledgments

Norman G. Finkelstein wishes to thank Ellen Adler, David Abraham, Rudolph Baldeo, Sara Bershtel, Roane Carey, Noam Chomsky, Samira Haj, Adele Oltman, Shifra Stern, Jack Trumpbour, and Cyrus Veeser for comments on an earlier draft. This essay is dedicated to the memory of his beloved parents, both survivors of the Warsaw Ghetto and the Nazi concentration camps: only a rational apprehension of what happened can give point to their martyrdom.

Ruth Bettina Birn wishes to acknowledge the collaboration of Dr. Volker Riess in the preparation and writing of this article.

Both authors wish to thank the staff of Metropolitan Books for their assistance and support.

*In the opinion, not of bad men, but
of the best men, no belief which is
contrary to truth can be really useful.*

JOHN STUART MILL

Contents

Part One

DANIEL JONAH

GOLDHAGEN'S

"CRAZY" THESIS

A Critique of *Hitler's Willing Executioners*

Norman G. Finkelstein

Rarely has a book with scholarly pretensions evoked as much popular interest as Daniel Jonah Goldhagen's study *Hitler's Willing Executioners: Ordinary Germans and the Holocaust.*[1] Every important journal of opinion printed one or more reviews within weeks of its release. *The New York Times,* for instance, featured multiple notices acclaiming Goldhagen's book as "one of those rare new works that merit the appellation landmark," "historic," and bringing to bear "corrosive literary passion." Although initial reviews were not uniformly positive, once the Goldhagen juggernaut proved unstoppable, even the

_____

1. New York, 1996.

dissenting media voices joined in the chorus of praise. An immediate national best-seller, *Hitler's Willing Executioners* was hailed in *Time* magazine's year-end issue as the "most talked about" and second best nonfiction book of 1996. Before long, Goldhagen was also an international phenomenon, creating an extraordinary stir in Germany.[2]

What makes the Goldhagen phenomenon so remarkable is that *Hitler's Willing Executioners* is not at all a learned inquiry. Replete with gross misrepresentations of the secondary literature and internal contradictions, Goldhagen's book is worthless as scholarship. The bulk of what follows documents this claim. But then, given its demonstrable flimsiness, we have to ask why the book has enjoyed such a clamorously popular reception. In the conclusion I speculate upon one possible explanation of this conspicuously puzzling fact.

---

2. *The New York Times,* 27 March, 2 April, 3 April 1996. *The New York Times Book Review* ran a somewhat less effusive notice (14 April 1996). *The New York Times Index* lists fully forty-two separate references to Goldhagen in 1996 alone. See *Time,* 23 December 1996. *The New York Review of Books* first gave *Hitler's Willing Executioners* a tepid notice but then ran a glowing piece in which it was acclaimed as "an original, indeed, brilliant contribution to the mountain of literature on the Holocaust" (18 April 1996, 28 November 1996). Initially running a hostile review, *The New Republic* subsequently featured Goldhagen's nine-page "reply to my critics" (29 April 1996, 23 December 1996). Crucial as it is to fully apprehending the Goldhagen phenomenon, the German reaction will not be considered in this essay. Deciphering its anomalies would require a much more intimate knowledge of the German cultural landscape than this writer possesses.

1

Before the Genocide

*Genocide was immanent in the conversation of German
society. It was immanent in its language and emotion.
It was immanent in the structure of cognition.*
HITLER'S WILLING EXECUTIONERS, 449

I.

In a seminal study published thirty-five years ago, *The
Destruction of the European Jews,* Raul Hilberg observed that
the perpetrators of the Nazi holocaust were "not different in
their moral makeup from the rest of the population. . . .
[T]he machinery of destruction was a remarkable cross-
section of the German population." These representative
Germans, Hilberg went on to say, performed their appointed
tasks with astonishing efficiency: "No obstruction stopped
the German machine of destruction. No moral problem
proved insurmountable. When all participating personnel
were put to the test, there were very few lingerers and almost
no deserters." Indeed, an "uncomfortably large number of

soldiers . . . delighted in death as spectators or as perpetrators."[3]

Long before Daniel Jonah Goldhagen's study, it was thus already known that "ordinary" Germans were Hitler's "willing" and not infrequently cruel "executioners."[4] The main distinction of Goldhagen's study is the explanation it purports to supply for what Hilberg called this "phenomenon of the greatest magnitude."[5] It is Goldhagen's thesis that the "central causal agent of the Holocaust" was the German people's enduring pathological hatred of the Jews (*Hitler's Willing Executioners* [hereafter *HWE*]: 9). To cite one typical passage:

> [A] demonological antisemitism, of the virulent racial variety, was the common structure of the perpetrators' cognition and of German society in general. The German perpetrators . . . were assenting mass executioners, men and women who, true to their own eliminationist antisemitic beliefs, faithful to their cultural antisemitic credo, considered the slaughter to be just. (*HWE:* 392–3)

There are no prima facie grounds for dismissing Goldhagen's thesis. It is not intrinsically racist or otherwise illegiti-

---

3. Raul Hilberg, *The Destruction of the European Jews* (New York, 1961). My page references will be to the three-volume "revised and definitive edition" published by Holmes and Meier in 1985: vol. iii, 1011, vol. i, 327; cf. vol. iii, 994. Cf. also Raul Hilberg, *Perpetrators, Victims, Bystanders* (New York, 1992), 28: "Whether they were in command or lowly placed, in an office or outdoors, they all did their part, when the time came, with all the efficiency they could muster." For initial reaction to Hilberg's damning portrait of German culpability, cf. Raul Hilberg, *The Politics of Memory* (Chicago, 1996), 124–6. In this text, *Nazi holocaust* refers to the actual historical event, *Holocaust* to its ideological distortion. This distinction will be clarified in the conclusion.

4. Hilberg specifically pointed to the Order Police—the subject of Goldhagen's study—as perpetrators whose "moral makeup" typified "Germany as a whole" (vol. iii, 1011).

5. Ibid.

mate. There is no obvious reason why a culture can't be fanatically consumed by hatred. One may further recall that, Goldhagen's claims to novelty notwithstanding, his argument is not altogether new. In the immediate aftermath of World War II, the genesis of the Final Solution was located in a twisted "German mind" or "German character."[6] The departure point of Holocaust literature is that Germans, nurtured on anti-Semitism, were thirsting for a "war against the Jews." On the eve of Hitler's ascension to power, wrote Lucy Dawidowicz, Germany was "a world intoxicated with hate, driven by paranoia, enemies everywhere, the Jew lurking behind each one." The complicity of Germans at every level of society in the Final Solution, Holocaust historian Steven T. Katz likewise argues, ineluctably "flowed" from their belief in the "parasitic vileness of 'the Jew.' "[7] This is also the dominant image of the Nazi extermination among Jews and in popular culture generally.

Bolstered as it is by a bulging scholarly apparatus, the audacious sweep of Goldhagen's thesis nonetheless merits emphasis. He argues that, for centuries, nearly every German was possessed of a homicidal animus toward Jews. Thus, he suggests that more than 80–90 percent of the German people would have relished the occasion to torture and murder Jews.[8]

---

6. For background and critical commentary, cf. Eric A. Zillmer et al., *The Quest for the Nazi Personality* (Hillsdale, NJ, 1995). Sampling a wide array of clinical data, the authors dismiss the "simplistic" notion of a "specific homicidal and clinically morbid" German personality (13). See also Ian Kershaw, *The Nazi Dictatorship* (New York, 1993), 6–7, 14.

7. Lucy Dawidowicz, *The War Against the Jews* (New York, 1975), 47; cf. 163–6; cf. also Lucy Dawidowicz, *The Holocaust and the Historians* (Cambridge, 1981), 11–12, 41, 59. Steven T. Katz, *The Holocaust in Historical Context* (Oxford, 1994), 10–11.

8. Goldhagen dissents from Christopher Browning's estimates that 10–20 percent of the German police battalions refused to kill Jews as "stretching the evi-

Goldhagen takes to task the "conventional explanations" that supposedly ignore the "identity of the victims": "That the victims were Jewish—according to the logic of these explanations—is irrelevant." Indeed, he declaims that we must "abandon the *assumption* that, by and large, Germans in the nineteenth and twentieth century were not antisemitic" (*HWE:* 13, 30–1, emphasis in original). In a rejoinder to critics, Goldhagen credits his own book as being the first to correct this misconception: "Most seem now to agree that anti-Semitism was a necessary cause of the Holocaust . . ." ("A Reply to My Critics," in *The New Republic,* 23 December 1996 [hereafter *Reply*]: 41). Yet, one is hard-pressed to name an account of the Nazi genocide that *doesn't* situate it within the context of German anti-Semitism.[9] Goldhagen's true distinction is to argue that German anti-Semitism was not only an integral but rather that it was *the* sufficient condition for perpetrating the extermination of the Jews: "With regard to the *motivational* cause of the Holocaust, for the vast majority of perpetrators, a monocausal explanation does suffice" (*HWE:* 416, emphasis in original; cf. 455, 582 n42).

The Hitlerite regime accordingly plays a subordinate role in Goldhagen's comprehension of the Final Solution. Inasmuch as the inclination for "killing" Jews "predated Nazi political power," the Nazis were "easily able to harness the perpetrators' preexisting antisemitism once Hitler gave the order to undertake the extermination" (*HWE:* 399, 463; cf. 418–9). All Hitler did was "unleash the pent-up antisemitic

---

dence" (*HWE:* 541 n68; cf. 551 n65). It is one of Goldhagen's central contentions that the police battalions were prototypical of the murderous German mind-set; cf. *HWE:* 181–5, 463ff.

9. Compare Saul Friedländer, "From Anti-Semitism to Extermination," in *Yad Vashem Studies,* XVI (Jerusalem, 1984), 7.

passion," "unshackle and thereby activate Germans' preexisting, pent-up antisemitism," and so on (*HWE:* 95, 442, 443). Leaving to one side the question of its veracity, this last formulation of Goldhagen's is still problematic. Consider that he repeatedly contradicts it. Had it not been for "Hitler's moral authority," Goldhagen observes, the "vast majority of Germans never would have contemplated" the genocide against the Jews (*Reply:* 42; cf. *HWE:* 446–7).[10] It was the Nazis' unprecedentedly "extreme and thoroughgoing . . . cognitive-moral revolution" that, Goldhagen suggests, produced Germany's "lethal political culture" (*HWE:* 456; cf. *Reply:* 42). Unaware that "these Germans were like no Germans they had ever known," Goldhagen explains, Soviet Jewry "initially greeted" the Nazi soldiers "obligingly and without hostility" (*HWE:* 587 n87). But if Goldhagen's thesis is correct, these Germans *were* like all other Germans.

On a related issue, Goldhagen dismisses the need for a comparative study by pointing up the centrality of Hitler's regime: "Whatever the antisemitic traditions were in other European countries, it was only in Germany that an openly and rabidly antisemitic movement came to power . . . that was bent upon turning antisemitic fantasy into state organized genocidal slaughter" (*HWE:* 419; cf. *Reply:* 43). Yet Goldhagen's account merely restates the problem: Why did "an openly and rabidly antisemitic movement" come to power in Germany and not elsewhere? The answer cannot be the uniqueness of German anti-Semitism. That simply returns us to the comparative

---

10. Not to be deterred by the hobgoblin of consistency, Goldhagen writes a couple of pages earlier: "By the time Hitler came to power, the model of Jews that was the basis of his anti-Semitism was shared by the vast majority of Germans" (*Reply:* 40).

question. True, Goldhagen argues: "Had there not been an economic depression in Germany, then the Nazis, in all likelihood, would never have come to power" (*Reply:* 42; cf. *HWE:* 87). But that just evades another obvious question: If Germans were so possessed by a fanatical anti-Semitism—more on which directly—why did "an openly and rabidly antisemitic movement" have to await an economic depression to attain power?

Indeed, *Hitler's Willing Executioners* is a monument to question-begging. Eschewing the claim that it is "inexplicable," Goldhagen sets as his objective to "explain why the Holocaust occurred, to explain how it could occur." He concludes that it "is explicable historically" (*HWE:* 5, 455). Goldhagen's thesis, however, neither renders the Nazi holocaust intelligible nor is it historical. For argument's sake, let us assume that Goldhagen is correct. Consumed by a ferocious loathing of the Jews, the German people jumped at Hitler's invitation to exterminate them. Yet the question still remains, Whence the hatred of Jews? A nation of genocidal racists is, after all, not exactly a commonplace.

On this crucial issue, Goldhagen sheds no light. Anti-Semitism, he suggests, was symptomatic of a much deeper German malaise. It served the Germans as a "moral rationale" for releasing "destructive and ferocious passions that are usually tamed and curbed by civilization" (*HWE:* 397). Yet, he explains neither why these normally quiescent passions burst forth in Germany nor why they were directed against the Jews. Goldhagen depicts anti-Semitism as the manifestation of a deranged state. The Germans were "pathologically ill . . . struck with the illness of sadism . . . diseased . . . tyrannical, sadistic," "psychopathic" (*HWE:* 397, 450, quoting a "keen diarist of the Warsaw Ghetto"), in thrall to "absolutely fantastical . . . beliefs that ordinarily only madmen have of others . . . [prone] to wild, 'magical thinking' " (*HWE:* 412), and so on.[11] Goldhagen never explains, however, why the Germans succumbed and why the Jews fell victim to this derangement.

In what is surely the book's most evocative analogy, Goldhagen compares the Germans to "crazy" Captain Ahab. Recalling Melville's memorable description of Ahab's insanely hateful state as he harpoons the whale, Goldhagen writes: "Germans' violent anger at the Jews is akin to the passion that drove Ahab to hunt Moby-Dick" (*HWE*: 398–9). Yet even if, as Goldhagen maintains, the Germans were "crazy" like Ahab, it still remains to explain what drove them to such a frenzied state. In Ahab's case, the motive is clear. Moby-Dick had earlier mangled him. To quote Melville from the passage Goldhagen excerpts: "It was revenge." But Goldhagen plainly does not believe the Jews inflicted violent injury on Germans. Indeed, he emphatically denies that Jews bear any responsibility for anti-Semitism: "The existence of antisemitism and the content of antisemitic charges . . . are fundamentally *not* a response to any objective evaluation of Jewish actions . . . antisemitism draws on cultural sources that are *independent* of the Jews' nature and actions" (*HWE*: 39, emphasis in original). In an almost comically circular argument, Goldhagen concludes that the Germans' Ahab-like loathing of the Jews originated in their loathing of the Jews: "Germans' antisemitism was the basis of their profound hatred of the Jews and the psychological impulse to make them suffer" (*HWE*: 584 n62; cf. 399).[12] This argument recalls one of Goldhagen's

---

11. An unwitting ironist, Goldhagen elsewhere in the book counsels: "Germans should not be caricatured" (*HWE*: 382).

12. In the endnote, Goldhagen cautions that his argument "obviously does not explain people's capacity for cruelty in the first place or the gratification many derive from it." Yet, what needs explaining is not the mechanisms of these sadistic impulses but, as noted above, why the Germans succumbed and why the Jews fell victim to them.

key theoretical insights: "The motivational dimension is the most crucial for explaining the perpetrators' willingness to act" (*HWE: 20*).

Goldhagen approvingly cites the *Sonderweg* argument that "Germany developed along a singular path, setting it apart from other western countries" (*HWE: 419*). But Goldhagen's thesis has precious little in common with this argument. Unlike the *Sonderweg* proponents, he never once anchors the deformations of the German character in temporal developments. Rather, the perverted German consciousness of Goldhagen's making floats above and persists despite history. Just how little Goldhagen's argument has in common with *any* school of history is pointed up by his conclusion that the Germans' "absurd beliefs . . . rapidly dissipated" after the Second World War (*HWE: 593–4 n53; cf. 582 n38*). Indeed, Germans today are "democrats, committed democrats."[13] Emerging from oblivion and enduring for centuries, the psy-

---

13. *Jewish Book News,* 25 April 1996, 39. For equivalent formulations, cf. *Reply:* 43, and Goldhagen's numerous interviews. For Goldhagen's pandering to Germans, see his lecture on receiving Germany's Democracy Prize, "Modell Bundesrepublik: National History, Democracy, and Internationalization in Germany," in *How to Learn from History* (Bonn, 1997). For example, he lavishes praise on the Federal Republic for having dealt "honestly with the least savory part of its past." (Significantly, he utters not a single word about the Federal Republic's egregious record on prosecuting the perpetrators of this "least savory part of its past.") His main scholarly pretense, however, is that, until *Hitler's Willing Executioners,* anti-Semitism was systematically ignored in German historiography on the Nazi holocaust. How then can he praise Germans for having dealt "honestly . . ."? Indeed, beyond earshot of his German audience, Goldhagen thus explained the popularity of his book in Germany: "Fifty years after the end of the war, many Germans want to have an honest reckoning with the past. They are not satisfied with the myths and misleading perspectives that have dominated public discussion of the Holocaust and given comfort and alibis to so many. . . . Even to raise many of the book's issues, whether in private or public, has until now been difficult. . . . Ultimately, this is why the book has resonated so positively. . . . People are sick of the myths and alibis" (Afterword to Vintage paperback edition [1997], 465–6).

chopathic German mind vanished again into oblivion in the space of a few decades. Thus Goldhagen renders the Nazi holocaust "explicable historically."

The merit of his thesis, Goldhagen contends, is that it recognizes that "each individual made choices about how to treat Jews." Thus, it "restores the notion of individual responsibility" (*Reply:* 38). Yet if Goldhagen's thesis is correct, the exact opposite is true. Germans bear no individual or, for that matter, collective guilt. After all, German culture was "radically different" from ours. It shared none of our basic values. Killing Jews could accordingly be done in "good conscience" (*HWE:* 15). Germans perceived Jews the way we perceive roaches. They did not know better. They could not know better. It was a homogeneously sick society. Moral culpability, however, presumes moral awareness. Touted as a searing indictment of Germans, Goldhagen's thesis is, in fact, their perfect alibi. Who can condemn a "crazy" people?

II.

Goldhagen deploys two analytically distinct strategies to prove his thesis. The first derives from his own primary research on the German perpetrators of the genocide. Goldhagen maintains that some of the Germans' actions "defy all of the conventional explanations" (*HWE:* 391). In particular, he argues that only a murderously anti-Semitic culture can account for their wanton cruelty (*Reply:* 38–9). Yet, it is not at all obvious why Goldhagen's thesis is more compelling than one that, say, includes the legacy of German anti-Semitism exacerbated by the incessant, inflammatory Jew-baiting of Nazi propaganda exacerbated by the brutalizing effects of a singularly barbarous war. It is perhaps true, as Goldhagen suggests, that such a "patchwork explanation" (*HWE:* 391) does not yet fully plumb the depths of German bestiality. But Goldhagen himself acknowledges that neither does his theory. Ultimately, he concedes, the immensity of German cruelty "remains hard to fathom" and "the extent and nature of German antisemitism" cannot explain it (*HWE:* 584 n62, 584 n65; cf. 399).

The second thrust of Goldhagen's argument is to demonstrate historically that German society was seething with virulent anti-Semitism on the eve of Hitler's ascension to power. The undertaking is a daunting one. Goldhagen relies almost entirely on the recent secondary literature on German anti-Semitism. He acknowledges that his analysis cannot be "definitive" because the data needed "simply do not exist" (*HWE:* 47). In reality, however, the research situation is even worse than that. Not a jot of this scholarship, profuse as it is, sustains Goldhagen's thesis. No serious German historian discounts the legacy of German anti-Semitism; none, however, maintains that German anti-Semitism was in itself sufficiently virulent to account for the Nazi genocide.[14] Indeed, this is one reason versions of Goldhagen's thesis have been discarded in serious scholarly inquiry. The task Goldhagen sets himself is to force the new evidence into the Procrustean bed of an obsolete theory. To meet this challenge, Goldhagen fashions a new model of anti-Semitism. Thomas Kuhn suggested that a new paradigm comes into existence when anomalies

---

14. In an astonishingly disingenuous endnote, Goldhagen writes that "it is indeed striking how little or non-existent the *evidence* is that . . . Germans' beliefs about Jews differed from the incessantly trumpeted Nazi one" (*HWE:* 593 n49, emphasis in original). For a sample of this "little or non-existent evidence," see section IV below.

crop up that the old one can no longer accommodate. The purpose of Goldhagen's new paradigm, however, is to make the anomalies fit the old one.

The essence of Goldhagen's new paradigm is what he calls "eliminationist antisemitism." Goldhagen situates German anti-Semitism along a continuous spectrum. At one extreme was the perception that Jews were vaguely different. At the other extreme was the perception that Jews were distinctly evil. Between these poles were various perceptions that Jews were more or less flawed. Sliding from one end of the spectrum to the other, the complementary German desire to eliminate an unappealing feature of the Jews rapidly turned into the desire to eliminate Jews altogether. *"The eliminationist mind-set,"* Goldhagen proclaims, *"tended towards an exterminationist one"* (*HWE:* 71, emphasis in original; cf. 23, 77, 444). Thus, any German who questioned the group loyalty or objected to the business practices of Jews was effectively a Nazi brute. Wedded as it was to an assimilationist version of the "eliminationist mind-set," even German liberalism inexorably led to Auschwitz.[15]

Rescuing an otherwise improbable thesis, "eliminationist antisemitism" serves as Goldhagen's deus ex machina. Indeed, using this device, it is not at all difficult to prove that nearly every German was a latent Hitler. It would also not be at all difficult to prove that nearly every white American is a latent Grand Wizard. How many white Americans do not harbor any negative stereotypes about black people? If Goldhagen is correct, we are all closet racial psychopaths. Why then did the Final Solution happen in Germany? If we all suffer from an "eliminationist mind-set" then the "eliminationist mind-set"

---

15. I will illustrate Goldhagen's procedures in the next sections.

cannot by itself account for what Goldhagen calls a "sui generis event" (*HWE:* 419).

Casting as a theoretical novelty the distinction between "type[s] of antisemitism," Goldhagen dismisses previous scholars who "typically . . . treated" anti-Semitism "in an un-differentiated manner." Before he came along, "a person [was] either an antisemite or not" (*HWE:* 34–5; cf. *Reply:* 41). Leaving aside the fact that the contrasts he proposes between, say, religious and racial or latent and manifest anti-Semitism are standard in the Nazi holocaust literature,[16] it is Goldhagen himself who radically undercuts all distinctions: on the "eliminationist" spectrum, every manifestation of anti-Semitism and even philo-Semitism "tend[s] strongly towards a genocidal 'solution' " (*HWE:* 494 n92).[17]

In this connection, Goldhagen's resolution of a key controversy in the Nazi holocaust literature is noteworthy. Histori-

---

16. Cf. Peter Pulzer, *The Rise of Political Anti-Semitism in Germany and Austria* (New York, 1964), 30, 70, and Ian Kershaw, *Popular Opinion and Political Dissent in the Third Reich* (Oxford, 1983), 231. Both are basic texts. Consider Goldhagen's other theoretical breakthroughs:

> [E]ach *source* of [antisemitism] is embedded in an extended metaphorical structure that automatically extends the domain of phenomena, situations, and linguistic usages relevant to the antisemitic compass in a manner paralleling the metaphorical structure itself. (*HWE:* 35, emphasis in original)

> All antisemitisms can be divided according to one essential dissimilitude which can be usefully thought of as being dichotomous (even if, strictly speaking, this may not be the case). (*HWE:* 37)

> Prejudice is a manifestation of people's (individual and collective) search for *meaning*. (*HWE:* 39, emphasis in original)

Comment is superfluous.

17. The counterpoint to Goldhagen's homogenization of the German perpetrators is his heterogenization of the Germans' victims. Thus, Goldhagen's discriminations to prove that Jewish suffering was unique (cf. *HWE:* 175, 294, 311ff., 340ff., 523 n1). Absolute German evil and absolute Jewish martyrdom are the reciprocal faces of Goldhagen's Manichaean paradigm. Projecting, Goldhagen discerns a "Manichaean model that undergirded much of Germans' thinking about Jews" (*HWE:* 62). I will consider the ideological functions of Goldhagen's paradigm in the conclusion.

ans have long disputed whether Hitler sought from the outset (the intentionalist school) or was pressed by circumstances (the functionalist school) to exterminate the Jews. To prove the intentionalist thesis, Goldhagen simply lumps Hitler's various initiatives together: they were *all* effectively genocidal. Thus, Hitler's preinvasion orders that limited the extermination of Soviet Jews to adult males was "still genocidal." His ghettoization and deportation schemes were "bloodlessly genocidal," "proto-genocidal," "psychologically and ideologically the functional, if not the eventual, actual equivalent of genocide," "quasi-genocidal," "bloodless equivalents of genocide," and so on. Even the destruction of Jewish synagogues during Kristallnacht was a "proto-genocidal assault . . . the psychic equivalent of genocide" (*HWE:* 141, 146, 147, 153, 421).[18] The very basis of the intentionalist-functionalist controversy, however, is that the distinction between riot, expulsion, and mass murder, on the one hand, and genocide, on the other, does count. Why else focus on Hitler's decision to initiate the Judeocide? Goldhagen's proof annuls the debate's central premise. It also annuls the central premise of his own book. If all these policies evidence genocidal intent, then genocidal intent is very far from uncommon in human history. Yet, Goldhagen maintains that "the Holocaust is . . . utterly new," and it is "crucial[ly]" the genocidal intent that makes it so (*HWE:* 5, *Reply:* 45).[19]

Once Goldhagen attends to the matter of distinctions, the bankruptcy of his explanatory model stands exposed. Thus, he

---

18. For a variation on this argument, which conflates verbal abuse with "deportation and physical violence," cf. *HWE:* 125.

19. Ironically, apologetic German historians like Ernst Nolte were reproached in the *Historikerstreit* for this selfsame collapsing of distinctions regarding genocide. Compare Peter Baldwin, "The *Historikerstreit* in Context," in Peter Baldwin (ed.), *Reworking the Past* (Boston, 1990), 7.

also enters the strong caveat that German "eliminationist anti-semitism" was equally compatible with a broad range of social outcomes. It was "multipotential." Indeed, "eliminationist antisemitism" could "obvious[ly]" culminate in everything from "total assimilation" to "total annihilation," with "verbal assault," "legal restraints," "physical assault," "physical separation in ghettos," and "forcible and violent expulsion" all being intermediate possibilities (*HWE:* 69, 70, 132–6, 444, 494 n92). These multiple options, Goldhagen further eluci-dates, "were rough functional equivalents from the vantage point of the perpetrators" (*HWE:* 135; cf. 70). Yet, if all these policy options were "rough functional equivalents" for the "eliminationist" mind-set, then the "eliminationist" mind-set plainly cannot account for the genocidal variant: it "tended toward" all, hence toward no particular one, of them. So capa-cious is his conceptual device, Goldhagen suggests, that it can explain in a "logical" manner the full gamut of unfolding Ger-man anti-Jewish policies (*HWE:* 444). True, it explains all of them; it also explains none.

III.

Goldhagen's survey of German anti-Semitism roughly divides at the Nazis' ascension to power.

Pre-Nazi Germany

In his introductory chapter, Goldhagen emphasizes an analyt-ical distinction: "Some antisemitisms become woven into the moral order of society; others do not." Theorizing that the for-mer are potentially more explosive, Goldhagen puts "the con-ception of Jews in medieval Christendom" in this category:

"[I]ts uncompromising non-pluralistic and intolerant view of the moral basis of society . . . held the Jews to violate the moral order of the world. . . . Jews came to represent . . . much of the evil in the world; they not only represented it but also came to be seen by Christians as being synonymous with it, indeed as being self-willed agents of evil" (*HWE:* 37–8; cf. 51). Alas, Goldhagen also argues that anti-Semitism was not at the core of premodern Christianity: "In medieval times . . . Jews were seen to be responsible for many ills, but they remained always somewhat peripheral, on the fringes, spatially and theologically, of the Christian world, not central to its understanding of the world's troubles. . . . [E]ven if the Jews were to disappear, the Devil, the ultimate source of evil, would remain" (*HWE:* 67; cf. 77). Apart from his theoretical insight—or perhaps insight*s*—Goldhagen skips quickly over the premodern era.

Except perhaps for an obscure, unpublished, thirty-year-old doctoral dissertation, Goldhagen acknowledges, the extant scholarly literature on modern German anti-Semitism does not reach his conclusions. If, however, the same findings are "reconceptualize[d]" in a "new analytical and interpretative framework," they do, he believes, sustain his novel thesis (*HWE:* 488 n17, 76–7; cf. *Reply:* 41). Summarizing his conclusions for the nineteenth century through World War I, Goldhagen writes:

> It is . . . incontestable that the fundamentals of Nazi anti-semitism . . . had deep roots in Germany, was part of the cultural cognitive model of German society, and was integral to German political culture. It is incontestable that racial antisemitism was the salient form of antisemitism in Germany and that it was broadly part of the public conversation of German society. It is incontestable that it had enormously wide and solid institutional and political

support in Germany at various times. . . . It is incontestable that this racial antisemitism which held the Jews to pose a mortal threat to Germany was pregnant with murder. (*HWE:* 74–5; cf. 77)

No serious historian doubts that anti-Semitism persisted in modern Germany. The question is, What were its scope and nature?[20] Goldhagen argues that anti-Semitism was ubiquitous in Germany. Yet German social democracy forcefully denounced anti-Semitism and, as the single largest political party (SPD), commanded the allegiance of fully one third the electorate by the early twentieth century. Not the working-class base, Goldhagen suggests, but only the "core of the socialist movement, its intellectuals and leaders," repudiated anti-Semitism. It was merely a "small [group]" (*HWE:* 74; cf. 72). The only source he cites is Peter Pulzer's *Jews and the German State,*[21] which enters no such qualification. Indeed, turning to Pulzer's authoritative companion study, *The Rise of Political Anti-Semitism in Germany and Austria,* we learn that "antisemitism drew little strength from . . . the working-class. . . . The [German worker] knew that national and religious arguments were at best irrelevant to a solution of his problems and at worst a deliberate attempt to cloud his view

---

20. In his rejoinder, Goldhagen downplays the import of this question: "Even if some would conclude that I am not entirely correct about the scope and character of German anti-Semitism, it does not follow that this would invalidate my conclusions . . . about the perpetration of the Holocaust, [which] logically can stand on its own and must be confronted directly." And again: "My assertions about the reach of anti-Semitism in Germany before the Nazi period is [*sic*] supported by the works of some of the most distinguished scholars of anti-Semitism. . . . Where I depart from some of them is not over the extent of anti-Semitism in Germany, but over its content and nature" (*Reply:* 40, 41). Yet, the "scope and character," "content and nature" of German anti-Semitism are not distinct from or subsidiary to but the very essence of his thesis.

21. Oxford, 1992.

of the 'real issues.' "[22] A compelling example of popular German anti-Semitism cited by Goldhagen is the recurrence of ritual murder accusations. "In Germany and the Austrian Empire," he reports, "twelve such trials took place between 1867 and 1914" (HWE: 63–4). Goldhagen cites Pulzer's *The Rise of Political Anti-Semitism in Germany and Austria.* Turning to the cited page, we find that Goldhagen has reversed the import of Pulzer's finding. The remainder of the sentence reads: "eleven of which collapsed although the trials were by jury."[23]

Quoting a scholarly study, Goldhagen recalls a "spontaneous, extremely broad-based, and genuine" petition campaign in Bavaria opposing the full equality of Jews. Yet in the corresponding note buried in the book's back pages, Goldhagen himself cites credible evidence that the campaign was carefully orchestrated by "priests and other anti-Jewish agitators" and that "many" signatories were "indifferent" to the Jews. Ian Kershaw adds that "many petitioners . . . knew little of any Jewish Question." Unfazed, Goldhagen concludes his endnote: "[B]ecause agitators could so easily induce them to antisemitic expression," the petition drive still proves "how antisemitic Bavarians were" (HWE: 61, 491 n51).[24]

Even if Goldhagen were able to prove that German culture was "axiomatically antisemitic" (HWE: 59), that in itself

---

22. Pulzer, *The Rise of Political Anti-Semitism in Germany and Austria,* 279–80.
23. Ibid., 71.
24. Kershaw, *Popular Opinion and Political Dissent in the Third Reich,* 229. Indeed, the study is marred throughout by Goldhagen's penchant for double bookkeeping. Thus, in the text's body Goldhagen implies that no police battalion member initially refrained from killing infants. Turning to the back of the book, we learn that, according to one member, "almost all the men" refused, and according to another, "as if by tacit agreement, the shooting of infants and small children was renounced by all the people." In the endnote Goldhagen grudgingly concedes that "undoubtedly, some of the men did shy away" (HWE: 216, 538 n37, n39).

would not yet prove that the German people strained at the bit to murder Jews. Thus, as seen above, Goldhagen also argues that German anti-Semitism was pervasively homicidal. Consider two more representative passages:

> By the end of the nineteenth century, the view that Jews posed extreme danger to Germany and that the source of their perniciousness was immutable, namely their race, and the consequential belief that the Jews had to be *eliminated* from Germany were extremely widespread in German society. The tendency to consider and propose the most radical form of elimination—that is, extermination—was already strong and had been given much voice. (*HWE:* 72, emphasis in original)

> [T]he cognitive model of Nazi antisemitism had taken shape well before the Nazis came to power, and . . . this model, throughout the nineteenth and early twentieth centuries, was also extremely widespread in all social classes and sectors of German society, for it was deeply embedded in German cultural and political life and conversation, as well as integrated into the moral structure of society. (*HWE:* 77)

Pulzer, however, maintains that only "a small, though growing, and noisy minority" even held that "Jews were a separate, inassimilable race." A second authority frequently cited by Goldhagen, Shulamit Volkov, similarly concludes that nineteenth-century German anti-Semitism did not "bring forth" the Nazi genocide. Indeed, it was "closer to the French version of that time than to later National Socialist positions."[25]

To document his thesis, Goldhagen repeatedly points to the proliferation of radically anti-Semitic literature in Germany.

---

25. Pulzer, *Jews and the German State,* 42, 14 (Volkov quote).

For instance, he cites the "startling" statistic that nineteen of fifty-one "prominent antisemitic writers" advocated the *"physical extermination of the Jews"* (*HWE:* 71, emphasis in original; cf. 64). One would perhaps also want to note that an overwhelming majority did not. As Goldhagen himself acknowledges two pages earlier: "[A] large percentage of the antisemites proposed no action at all." Goldhagen deems this last fact "astonishing"—but it would be astonishing only if his thesis were true. Goldhagen also never asks who read this literature. Scoring Germany as the birthplace and headquarters of "scientific" anti-Semitism, Eva Reichmann nonetheless cautions that "an anti-Semitic literature does not of necessity prove a wide anti-Semitic response among the public."[26]

Ill-suited to his thesis, the scholarly evidence is recast by Goldhagen with the aid of his novel methodology.[27] Thus,

---

26. Eva G. Reichmann, *Hostages of Civilization* (London, 1950), 154. Cf. Sarah Gordon, *Hitler, Germans, and the "Jewish Question"* (Princeton, NJ, 1984), 27.

27. I will not elucidate all of Goldhagen's methodological points on contemporary anti-Semitism. These include:

> While its cognitive content was adopting new forms in the service of "modernizing" antisemitism, of harmonizing it with the new social and political landscape of Germany, the existing cultural cognitive model about Jews provided a remarkable underlying constancy to the elaborated cultural and ideological pronouncements. (*HWE:* 53–4)

> In "functional" terms, the changing manifest content of antisemitism could be understood, in one sense, to have been little more than the handmaiden of the pervasive anti-Jewish animus that served to maintain and give people a measure of coherence in the modern world. . . . (*HWE:* 54)

> Previously, a welter of antisemitic charges and understandings of the source of the Jews' perniciousness had characterized the outpouring of anti-Jewish sentiment since the "Jewish Problem" had become a central political theme as a reaction to the movement for their emancipation. (*HWE:* 66)

> The cognitive model of ontology that underlay the essential, racist Volkish worldview contradicted and did not admit the Christian one that had held sway for centuries. (*HWE:* 68)

These are typical of the "insights and theories of the social sciences" that Goldhagen says "inform" his enterprise, unlike the criticism that "betrays a fundamental misunderstanding of the social scientific method" (*Reply:* 38–9, 43).

Goldhagen suggests that any German who believed that Jews constituted a "religion, nation, political group, or race" and thus were an "alien body within Germany," or that Jews engaged in "underhanded" or "parasitic" business activities fell on the eliminationist spectrum gliding to murder (*HWE:* 55–7, 64–73).[28] Leaving to one side that this classificatory system would yield a majority of racial psychopaths in any ethnically riven society, the identical image of Jews as a "nation" or "race" that was "alien" to and "parasitical" on European society was also a staple of Zionist ideology. Indeed, as one Zionist historian copiously documents, "the Jewish self-criticism so widespread among the German Zionist intelligentsia often seemed dangerously similar to the plaints of the German anti-Semites."[29] Does that make all Zionists homicidal anti-Semites as well? Pressed into Goldhagen's conceptual meat grinder, even German "liberals," "philosemites," and "progressives," with their ambivalent prescriptions for Jewish emancipation, emerge as racial psychopaths. Thus, Goldhagen reckons that Enlightenment Germans were "antisemites in sheep's clothing," "philosemitic antisemites," in thrall to the "assimilationist version of the eliminationist mind-set," etc. (*HWE:* cf. 56–9, 70, 74, 78). Small wonder that Goldhagen is able to prove that Germany was a nation of murderous Jew-haters.

For all its social turbulence, modern pre-Hitler Germany witnessed only episodic spasms of anti-Jewish violence.

---

28. For Goldhagen's recourse to this genre of argument for the Nazi period, cf. *HWE:* 106, 113–15, 126, 431.

29. Joachim Doron, "Classic Zionism and Modern Anti-Semitism: Parallels and Influences (1883–1914)," in *Studies in Zionism* (Autumn 1983), 169–204 (quote at 171). Cf. Norman G. Finkelstein, *Image and Reality of the Israel-Palestine Conflict* (London, 1995), chap. 1.

Indeed, there was no equivalent of the riots that attended the Dreyfus Affair in France or the pogroms in Russia. If Germany was brimming with pathological anti-Semites, why did Jews so rarely suffer their wrath? Alas, Goldhagen only briefly touches on this—for his thesis—plainly pivotal question. He writes: "As powerful and potentially violent as the anti-semitism was, . . . the state would not allow it to become the basis of collective social action of this sort. Wilhelmine Germany would not tolerate the organized violence for which the antisemites appeared to long" (*HWE:* 72). Yet, why was the State immune to the pathological anti-Semitism infecting the German body politic? Indeed, winning the 1893 election, the Conservative party, which according to Goldhagen was "thoroughly antisemitic," along with allied avowedly anti-Semitic parties, proved a force to reckon with in the State (*HWE:* 56, 74–6). Why did these violent anti-Semites "not tolerate" anti-Semitic violence?

Disobeying orders that they opposed, the Germans did not, according to Goldhagen, blindly defer to State authority. Indeed, if the State violated a normative value, "ordinary citizens" entered into "open rebellion" against, and "battled in the streets . . . in defiance of . . . and in order to overthrow it" (*HWE:* 381–2). Goldhagen further maintains that all the non-governmental centers of power in Germany—what he calls its "Tocquevillian substructure"—were packed with insane Jew-haters (*HWE:* 59–60, 72–4). If they were thus driven by fanatical anti-Semitism that was the German "cultural norm" (*HWE:* 61), the German people should have risen up against the Wilhelmine state that was shielding the Jews. Jewish blood should have been flowing in German streets. Luckily for the Jews, but unluckily for Goldhagen's thesis, this never happened. Ironically, the only "continual legislative and parliamentary battles," "bitter political fights," etc. Goldhagen chronicles were over Jewish emancipation (*HWE:* 56). If, as Goldhagen writes in the very same paragraphs, the "vast majority" of Germans were "thoroughly antisemitic," why was there such intense political discord on the Jewish Question?

Goldhagen acknowledges only parenthetically that, for all the entrenched anti-Semitism, modern German Jews experienced a "meteoric rise from pariah status" (*HWE:* 78). Indeed, German Jewry at the century's turn—recalls one historian— "thrived in this atmosphere of imperfect toleration; their coreligionists throughout the world . . . looked to them for support and leadership."[30] Goldhagen wisely does not even try to reconcile the "meteoric rise" of German Jews with the thesis that Germany was seething with psychopathic anti-Semitism.

Saturated with Jew-hatred, Weimar Germany was, according to Goldhagen, all of a piece. Thus "virtually every major institution and group . . . was permeated by antisemitism," "nearly every political group in the country shunned the Jews," "Jews, though ferociously attacked, found virtually no defenders . . . ," "the public conversation about Jews was almost wholly negative," etc. (*HWE:* 82–4).

It is true that anti-Semitism persisted in the Weimar era. Goldhagen recalls the "Aryan paragraphs" that restricted Jewish entry into universities and student organizations (*HWE:* 83). Yet, Jews in England and the United States suffered from similar disabilities. Popular anti-Semitic violence occasionally flared up during the years 1917–1923 when German society tottered on the brink of total collapse. Once the new regime

---

30. Donald L. Niewyk, *The Jews in Weimar Germany* (Baton Rouge, 1980), 9.

stabilized, however, almost all vandalization of Jewish property was connected with the Nazis. Unlike Goldhagen, Pulzer reports that the Social-Democratic party proved during Weimar "a committed opponent of organized anti-Semitism," and Niewyk reports that "the penetration of anti-Jewish opinions into the organized Socialist working class was kept to an unmeasurable minimum." To document that the "SPD did little to attack the Nazis' antisemitism," Goldhagen cites Donna Harsch's study *German Social Democracy and the Rise of Nazism* (*HWE:* 497 n16). Turning to the cited page, we learn that, although the SPD did react defensively to slurs that it was beholden to the Jewish community, "all Social Democrats" proved "consistent" in their "advocacy of the civil rights of German and East European Jews."[31]

Goldhagen's monochromatic thumbnail sketch also completely omits the remarkable successes registered by German Jews. Occupying a salient place in German life, Weimar Jewry assembled a record of achievements in the arts, politics, and the economy rivaled only by that of American Jewry after World War II. "Had the German population been uniquely rabid in its hatred," Sarah Gordon reasonably concludes, "it is inconceivable that Jews could have fared so well, especially compared to Jews in other nations."[32]

---

31. Michael H. Kater, "Everyday Anti-Semitism in Prewar Nazi Germany: The Popular Bases," in *Yad Vashem Studies,* XVI (Jerusalem, 1984), 133; Niewyk, *The Jews in Weimar Germany,* 51, 69 (working class quote), 70; Pulzer, *The Rise of Political Anti-Semitism in Germany and Austria,* 325; Pulzer, *Jews and the German State,* 261 (SPD quote), 344–5; Donna Harsch, *German Social Democracy and the Rise of Nazism* (Chapel Hill, 1993), 70.

32. Gordon, *Hitler, Germans, and the "Jewish Question,"* 48. For a balanced presentation of German Jewry during the Weimar years, cf. esp. Donald L. Niewyk's study.

Shouting from the rooftop his maniacal hatred of the Jews, Hitler fully and incessantly apprised the German people, according to Goldhagen, of his genocidal plans. "In his writing, speeches, and conversation," Goldhagen states, "Hitler was direct and clear. Germany's enemies at home and abroad were to be destroyed or rendered inert. No one who heard or read Hitler could have missed this clarion message" (*HWE:* 86). And again: "Rarely has a national leader so openly, frequently, and emphatically announced an apocalyptic intention—in this case, to destroy Jewish power and even the Jews themselves—and made good on his promise" (*HWE:* 162; cf. 424).

Yet, Goldhagen adduces only three pieces of evidence for the period through the eve of World War II to document this claim: the notorious passage from *Mein Kampf,* which perhaps few Germans read and even fewer took literally; a speech "at the beginning of [Hitler's] political career" in 1920 when he was "still politically obscure"; and Hitler's conditional and ambiguous January 1939 "prophecy," which was largely ignored by a German public preoccupied with the impending war (*HWE:* 86, 142, 162, 424–5).[33]

---

33. William Brustein, *The Logic of Evil* (New Haven, 1996), 51, reports that "relatively few people read *Mein Kampf*" before 1933. Albert Speer claimed never to have read it; his biographer is unsure (Albert Speer, *Inside the Third Reich* [New York, 1970], 19, 122, 509; Gitta Sereny, *Albert Speer* [New York, 1995], 183, 302, 590–1). Although the notorious passage from *Mein Kampf* is not strictly genocidal—Hitler speculates that if "twelve or fifteen thousand . . . Hebrew corrupters of the people had been held under poison gas," Germany might have won World War I—Philippe Burrin, *Hitler and the Jews* (London, 1994), convincingly demonstrates that these musings do shed important light on Hitler's genocidal aims. For the linguistic ambiguities of and indifferent public reception to Hitler's January 1939 "prophecy," cf. Gordon, *Hitler, Germans, and the "Jewish*

Hitler's public statements have been subject to numerous analyses. None confirm Goldhagen's depiction. Indeed, yet again directly contradicting his own thesis, Goldhagen reports that Hitler "prudently would not repeat in public" his explicitly genocidal aims "after he had achieved national prominence." Goldhagen also validates Göbbels's boast in 1944 that, before seizing power, the Nazis "had not made their ultimate intentions known publicly" (Goldhagen's paraphrase) (*HWE:* 425, 589 n13). The actual documentary record for the period through 1939 shows that: (1) Hitler's earliest speeches were pervasively anti-Semitic; (2) realizing, however, that "anti-Marxism had a wider potential appeal than the mere repetition of anti-Jewish paroxysms of hate" (Kershaw), Hitler muted the anti-Semitism once he entered public life in 1923; (3) anti-Semitism figured only marginally in Hitler's speeches during the years immediately preceding his electoral triumph; (4) upon taking power and until the eve of World War II, Hitler publicly announced as his "ultimate goal" (Domarus) not the annihilation but the forced emigration of the Jews.[34]

Question," 133; Ian Kershaw, *The "Hitler Myth"* (Oxford, 1987), 240–2; Hans Mommsen, "The Realization of the Unthinkable," in Gerhard Hirschfeld (ed.), *The Policies of Genocide* (London, 1986), 134–5 n36.
34. Norman H. Baynes (ed.), *The Speeches of Adolf Hitler, April 1922–August 1939* (New York, 1969), 721; Brustein, *The Logic of Evil,* 58; Max Domarus (ed.), *Hitler: Speeches and Proclamations, 1932–1945* (Wauconda, IL, 1990), 37, 40 (quote); Saul Friedländer, *Nazi Germany and the Jews* (New York, 1997), 72, 95–7, 101–4 (Friedländer puts more stress on Hitler's public anti-Semitism throughout the 1920s but concurs that in the early 1930s "the Jewish theme indeed became less frequent in his rhetoric"); Sarah Gordon, *Hitler, Germans, and the "Jewish Question,"* 84, 129; Kershaw, *The "Hitler Myth,"* 230–5 (quote on 231); Niewyk, *The Jews in Weimar Germany,* 54. For the period January 1932–March 1933, there is no mention at all of Jews in any of Hitler's speeches collected in Domarus's standard edition. The main negative theme is anti-Bolshevism and -Marxism. In Baynes's earlier collection of Hitler extracts that "practically exhausts the material on the subject" of the Jews, the only item before 1933 is an interview with *The Times* of London in which Hitler, repudiating "violent anti-

"Even during the War when his machinery of destruction was running at top capacity," Max Domarus recalls, Hitler

> confined his remarks on a massacre of Jews to threats within the scope of his foreign policy, knowing only too well that such an openly propagated program of extermination was certain to meet with resistance from the majority of the German people and the bulk of his party followers.[35]

Yet, Goldhagen writes: "Hitler announced many times, emphatically, that the war would end in the extermination of the Jews. The killing met with general understanding, if not approval." The endnote refers readers to Max Domarus (*HWE:* 8, 477 n10).

The Nazi genocide, Goldhagen elucidates, was "given shape and energized by a leader, Hitler, who was adored by the vast majority of the German people, a leader who was known to be committed wholeheartedly to the unfolding, brutal eliminationist program" (*HWE:* 419). Pointing up "Hitler's enormous popularity and the legitimacy that it helped engender for the regime," Goldhagen elsewhere refers readers to Ian Kershaw's important study *The "Hitler Myth"* (*HWE:* 512 n2). Yet Goldhagen omits altogether Kershaw's main finding— that anti-Semitism never figured centrally in Hitler's mass appeal. Thus Kershaw typically writes:

Semitism," declares that he "would have nothing to do with pogroms" (726). Although "unjust and harsh," Domarus recalls, Hitler's forced emigration scheme was hardly unprecedented even in the modern world (40).

35. Domarus, *Hitler: Speeches and Proclamations,* 37; cf. Kershaw, *The "Hitler Myth,"* 243–4; Lothar Kettehacker, "Hitler's Final Solution and Its Rationalization," in Gerhard Hirschfeld (ed.), *The Policies of Genocide* (London, 1986), 83; Mommsen, "The Realization of the Unthinkable," 108–11.

Anti-Semitism, despite its pivotal place in Hitler's "world view," was of only secondary importance in cementing the bonds between Fuhrer and people which provided the Third Reich with its popular legitimation and basis of plebiscitary acclamation. At the same time, the principle of excluding the Jews from German society was itself widely and increasingly popular, and Hitler's hatred of the Jews—baleful in its threats but linked to the condoning of lawful, "rational" action, not the unpopular crude violence and brutality of the Party's "gutter" elements—was certainly an acceptable component of his popular image, even if it was an element "taken on board" rather than forming a centrally motivating factor for most Germans.

Indeed, "during the 1930s . . . when his popularity was soaring to dizzy heights," Kershaw underlines, Hitler "was extremely careful to avoid public association with the generally unpopular pogrom-type anti-Semitic outrages."[36]

Like Hitler's public persona, the electoral cycle culminating in the Nazi victory has been closely scrutinized by historians. These contests were a uniquely sensitive barometer of the fluctuations in German popular opinion. The consensus of the scholarly literature is that anti-Semitism did not figure centrally in the Nazis' ultimate success at the polls.[37] Before the

---

36. Kershaw, The "Hitler Myth," 46–7, 152, 154, 161, 230, 233, 235–8, 239 (second quote), 250 (first quote), 252; cf. Kershaw, Popular Opinion and Political Dissent in the Third Reich, 273. In light of Goldhagen's claim cited below that the Nazi regime was fundamentally "consensual," it also bears repeating Kershaw's "obvious" caveat that "the Nazi regime was a terroristic dictatorship—in a literal sense, a terrifying regime—which knew no bounds in the repression of its perceived enemies" (The Nazi Dictatorship, 171, emphasis in original).

37. William Sheridan Allen, The Nazi Seizure of Power (New York, 1984), 84, 218; Brustein, The Logic of Evil, xii, 51, 57–8, 88, 180–1; Thomas Childers, The Nazi Voter (Chapel Hill, 1983), 43, 262–8; Gordon, Hitler, Germans, and the "Jewish Question," 29ff., 45, 68–71, 82, 299; Richard Hamilton, Who Voted for Hitler?

massive economic depression sent German society reeling, neither the Nazis nor any of the other radical anti-Semitic parties were able to garner more than a minuscule percentage of the votes. Even as late as 1928, only 2.8 percent of the German electorate cast ballots for the Nazi party. The subsequent spectacular upswing in the Nazis' electoral fortunes was due overwhelmingly to the solutions they proposed for Germany's economic crisis. Not the Jews but Marxism and Social Democracy served as the prime scapegoats of Nazi propaganda. Anti-Semitism was not altogether jettisoned by the Nazis; it did not, however, account for the core of their support. In perhaps the single most illuminating interpretive study of the Nazi phenomenon, Eva Reichmann subtly elucidates this relationship:

> In an excessively complicated situation Nazism offered to a society in full disintegration a political diet whose disastrous effects this society was no longer able to realize. People felt that it contained titbits for every palate. The titbits were, so to speak, coated with anti-Semitism. . . . But it was not the covering for the sake of which they were greedily swallowed. . . . The wrapping in which the new security, the new self-assurance, the exculpation, the permission to hate was served might equally well have had another colour and another spice.

(Princeton, NJ, 1982), 363–9, 377–8, 418, 421–2, 607 n46; and Eva Reichmann, *Hostages of Civilization,* 190, 229–36. It is not at all even clear that anti-Semitism figured prominently in the motives for joining the Nazi party before, let alone after, Hitler's victory; cf. esp. Peter H. Merkl, *Political Violence Under the Swastika* (Princeton, NJ, 1975), 499–500. To illustrate that the crudely anti-Semitic SA was "representative of a significant percentage of the German people" during the Nazi years, Goldhagen recalls that its membership "was approximately 10 percent of the German civilian male population of the age cohorts on which the SA drew" (*HWE:* 95). Leaving to one side that a tip does not always prove an iceberg, Goldhagen observes elsewhere that "many non-ideological reasons" induced Germans to join Nazi organizations (*HWE:* 208).

The "conclusiveness of this analogy," Reichmann significantly adds, is "confirmed" by the absence of popular anti-Semitic malice prior to the Nazi victory:

> If those people who, under the influence of anti-Semitic propaganda, had been moved by outright hatred of the Jews, their practical aggression against them would have been excessive after the Jews had been openly abandoned to the people's fury. Violence would not then have been limited to the organised activities of Nazi gangs, but would have become endemic in the whole people and seriously endangered the life of every Jew in Germany. This, however, did not happen. Even during the years in which the party increased by leaps and bounds, spontaneous terrorist assaults on Jews were extremely rare. . . . In spite of the ardent efforts of the [Nazi party], the boycott against Jewish shopkeepers and professional men before the seizure of power was negligible, although this would have been an inconspicuous and safe way of demonstrating one's anti-Jewish feeling. From all this all but complete lack of practical anti-Semitic reactions at a time when the behavior of the public was still a correct index to its sentiments, it can only be inferred that the overwhelming majority of the people did not feel their relations to the Jewish minority as unbearable.[38]

Goldhagen dispatches the crucial cycle of elections culminating in the Nazi victory in one page. He highlights that, in the July 1932 election (the Nazis' best showing in an open contest), "almost *fourteen million* Germans, 37.4 percent of the voters, cast their lots for Hitler" (*HWE:* 87, emphasis in orig-

---

38. Reichmann, *Hostages of Civilization,* 231–3. Long out of print, this luminous work should be reissued.

inal). He might also have highlighted that more than *twenty-three million* Germans, 62.6 percent of the voters, did not cast their lot for Hitler. "There is no doubt," Goldhagen concludes, "that Hitler's virulent, lethal-sounding antisemitism did not at the very least deter Germans by the millions from throwing their support to him" (*HWE:* 497 n22). This finding, however, feebly sustains Goldhagen's thesis. If, as Goldhagen claims, the Germans were straining at the bit to murder the Jews, and if, as he claims, Hitler promised to "unleash" them if elected, then Germans should have voted for Hitler not despite but *because of* his anti-Semitism. Not even Goldhagen, however, pretends this was the case. Indeed, Goldhagen acknowledges that "many people . . . welcomed Nazism while disliking certain of its aspects—as transient excrescences upon the body of the Party which Hitler . . . would slough off as so many alien accretions" (*HWE:* 435). This was precisely the case with Nazi anti-Semitism.[39] Finally, to demonstrate Hitler's greater popularity right after the seizure of power, Goldhagen recalls that the throttling of all dissent "did not deter voters, but increased the Nazi vote to over seventeen million people" in March 1933 (*HWE:* 87). One may have supposed that this increment in Nazi votes was perhaps *because* all dissent was throttled. Imagine if, to demonstrate the Communist regime's growing popular appeal, a Soviet historian argued that massive repression "did not deter, but increased the vote for Stalin to over. . . ." It is doubtful that even *Pravda* would have noticed such a book.

---

39. Childers, *The Nazi Voter,* 267.

IV.

The Nazi Years, 1933–1939

In her study of Nazism, Eva Reichmann observes that the "spontaneous" German attitude toward Jews can no longer be gauged after Hitler's ascension to power. Totalitarian rule corrupted Germans.[40] Goldhagen disagrees. Consistent with his "monocausal explanation," Goldhagen maintains that the Nazi regime's propaganda and repressive apparatuses did not do special injury to German-Jewish relations.

"It must be emphasized," Goldhagen writes, "that in no sense did the Nazis 'brainwash' the German people." Rather, the Germans were already in thrall to a "hallucinatory, demonized image of Jews" long before Hitler came on the scene (*HWE:* 594 n56; for a similar argument for the war years, cf. 251–2). Why then did the Nazi regime invest so much of its resources in fomenting Jew-hatred? Goldhagen recalls, for instance, that "the most consistent, frequently acted upon and pervasive German governmental policy" was "constant, ubiquitous, antisemitic vituperation issued from . . . public organs, ranging from Hitler's own speeches, to never-ending installments in Germany's radio, newspapers, magazines, and journals, to films, to public signage and verbal fusillades, to schoolbooks." Indeed, Goldhagen himself stresses that this "incessant antisemitic barrage" took an "enormous toll" not only on Jews but "also on Germans," and was aimed at "preparing Germans for still more drastic eliminationist measures" (*HWE:* 136, 124, 137).

---

40. Reichmann, *Hostages of Civilization,* 231, 261 n380.

Hitler's Willing Executioners is in fact replete with illustrations, cited approvingly by Goldhagen, that Nazi Jew-baiting *did* poison German sensibilities. Germans embraced anti-Semitism, an Einsatzkommando member confesses, because "it was hammered into us, during the years of propaganda, again and again, that the Jews were the ruin of every *Volk* in the midst of which they appear and that peace would reign in Europe only . . . when the Jewish race is exterminated" (*HWE:* 442). Popular anti-Semitism "was, after all, no surprise," a German Jew explained in 1942. "Because for nearly ten years the inferiority and harmfulness of the Jews has been emphasized in every newspaper, morning and evening, in every radio broadcast and on many posters, etc., without a voice in favor of the Jews being permitted to be raised" (*HWE:* 449). "I believed the propaganda that all Jews were criminals and subhumans," a former murderous police battalion member discloses, "and that they were the cause of Germany's decline after the First World War" (*HWE:* 179). "Nazi schooling produced a generation of human beings in Nazi Germany so different from normal American youth," an American educator recalls, "that mere academic comparison seems inane" (*HWE:* 27).

Indeed, Goldhagen's crowning piece of evidence confutes the book's central thesis. "In what may be the most significant and illuminating testimony given after the war," Goldhagen reports, an "expert legal brief" submitted at Nuremberg argued that the Einsatzgruppen "really believed" that Germany was locked in mortal combat with the Jewish agents of a Bolshevik conspiracy. Quoting from this "all but neglected" document, Goldhagen locates the "source" of these psychotic beliefs not in a murderously anti-Semitic German culture but in Nazi propaganda: ". . . it cannot be doubted that National

Socialism had succeeded to the fullest extent in convincing public opinion and furthermore *the overwhelming majority of the German people* of the identity of bolshevism and Jewry" (*HWE*: 393, Goldhagen's emphasis). Goldhagen seems totally unaware that he has just highlighted his "monocausal explanation" of the Nazi genocide into oblivion.[41]

Citing the findings of Robert Gellately, "the foremost expert on the Gestapo," Goldhagen reports that only a tiny handful of Germans were prosecuted for verbally dissenting from Nazi anti-Semitism. According to Goldhagen, this German silence cannot, however, be credited to repression. Contrary to widespread belief, Goldhagen maintains, the Hitlerian state was benign. The Nazis ruled "without massive coercion and violence." The regime "was, on the whole, consensual." Germans generally "accepted the system and Hitler's authority as desirable and legitimate" (*HWE*: 132, 429–30, 456).

Yet Gellately situates his findings in a radically different context from Goldhagen's. This "foremost expert on the Gestapo" proceeds "from the assumption that fear was indeed prevalent among the German people." To pretend otherwise, he asserts, is "foolish." Denunciation to settle private scores

---

41. Goldhagen's citation of this document is doubly ironic. Not only does it undercut his claim about the inefficacy of Nazi propaganda (a large chunk of the brief is devoted to the pernicious impact of "governmental propaganda in a totalitarian state"), but it also undercuts his claim about restoring the dimension of individual responsibility. Seeking to mitigate the culpability of the Einsatzgruppen commanders, the brief lent support to a kind of temporary insanity plea: "The defendants . . . were obsessed with a psychological delusion based on a fallacious idea concerning the identity of the aims of bolshevism and the political role of Jewry in eastern Europe." Although effectively endorsed by Goldhagen, this last defense was—fortunately for justice's sake—rejected by the Military Tribunal. *Trials of War Criminals Before the Nuernberg Military Tribunals,* vol. iv, "The Einsatzgruppen Case" (Washington, DC), 342, 344, 350, 354, 463–4.

was rampant. Especially vulnerable were Germans critical of Nazi anti-Semitism. With the promulgation of the 1935 Nuremberg Laws, "anyone friendly to Jews could be denounced on suspicion of having illicit relationships." Thus "numerous" Germans "in the employ of Jews or in some kind of business contact with them had brushes with the Gestapo when they persisted in these relations or expressed the mildest kinds of solidarity with the persecuted." Indeed, more often than not transgressions were summarily dealt with: "When it came to enforcing racial policies destined to isolate Jews, there can be no doubt that the wrath of the Gestapo knew no bounds, often dispensing with even the semblance of legal procedures. It is important to be reminded of the 'legal' and 'extra-legal' terror brought down on the heads of those who would not otherwise comply." "Sometimes . . . they were driven to suicide." Given the scope of the repression, Gellately suggests, care must be exercised not to infer too much from the Gestapo files. They "may well underestimate the degree of rejection of Nazi anti-Semitism." Germans "would be foolhardy to speak openly about reservations they might have on that score when brought in for interrogation." Moreover, "if they were never caught, hence never turned over to the Gestapo, there would be no official record of their activities. In addition, most of the files of those who were caught were destroyed."

Germans generally "accommodated themselves to the official line," Gellately nonetheless suggests, "and to all intents and purposes, did not stand in the way of the persecution of the Jews." It was, however, an acquiescence borne not of fanatical hatred but significantly of fear: "Being turned into the authorities for the smallest sign of non-compliance was too common not to have struck anxiety in the hearts of anyone who might under other circumstances have found no fault with the Jews."[42]

Dissenting, Goldhagen maintains that behind the German silence was not at all fear but "ideological congruity" with the murderous Nazi project (*HWE:* 591 n27). Accordingly, in his overview of the Nazi era, Goldhagen writes:

> Whatever else Germans thought about Hitler and the Nazi movement, however much they might have detested aspects of Nazism, the vast majority of them subscribed to the underlying Nazi model of Jews and in this sense (as the Nazis themselves understood) were "Nazified" in their view of Jews.

None of the copious relevant scholarship, Goldhagen acknowledges in the corresponding endnote, reaches his conclusions. Rather, Goldhagen leans on a "theoretical [and] analytical account of antisemitism" and an understanding of "the nature of cognitions, beliefs, and ideologies and their relation to action" (*HWE:* 87, 497–8 n24). Without his novel methodology, Goldhagen is indeed no more able to prove his thesis for the period after Hitler's ascension to power than he was for the period before it.

Goldhagen recalls the degrading and onerous proscriptions on Jewish life in Nazi Germany. He cites, for example, the barring of Jews from public facilities (e.g., swimming pools, public baths), the exclusion of Jews from prestigious professional associations and institutions (e.g., medicine, law, higher education) and later much of the economy, the posting of signs

---

42. Robert Gellately, *The Gestapo and German Society* (Oxford, 1990), 111, 129, 135–6, 146–7, 160–1, 171, 172, 177, 179, 186–7, 205–7, 213, 256.

that pointed up the Jews' pariah status (e.g., "Jews Not Wanted Here," "Entry Forbidden to Jews"), etc. (*HWE:* 91–3, 96–7, 124–5, 137–8).

Implemented "with the approval of the vast majority of people," these measures evinced, according to Goldhagen, the "Germans' eliminationist intent" (*HWE:* 422, 93). The actual record, however, is rather more complex.[43] Acting narrowly on their economic self-interest, Germans generally supported Nazi anti-Jewish initiatives from which they stood to gain materially and opposed Nazi anti-Jewish initiatives from which they stood to lose materially. Socially restrictive Nazi initiatives initially got a lukewarm reception. Goldhagen suggests otherwise. Citing Gellately, he reports that "Germans posted signs" with anti-Jewish prohibitions (*HWE:* 91–2). Turning to the cited page, we learn that the campaign was orchestrated "by local hotheads in the Nazi movement," with an opportunist German occasionally joining in. Succumbing, however, to the combined pressures of propaganda and repression, most Germans, already more or less disposed to anti-Semitic appeals, did come to endorse, with relative ease if not

---

43. A brief word about sources. Research on popular opinion in Nazi Germany relies mainly on reports secretly dispatched by the SPD underground and internal files of the Nazi police (Gestapo, SD). Goldhagen cautions that SPD reports "should be read with circumspection" because the "agents were obviously eager and ideologically disposed to find among the German people . . . evidence of dissent from the Nazi regime and its policies" (*HWE:* 509 n162; cf. 106). Oddly, he does not enter a comparable caveat in the reverse sense for the Gestapo reports, which are repeatedly cited by him to document popular German anti-Semitism (e.g., *HWE,* 98, 121). In any event, the issue of reliability has already been thoroughly explored. The consensus is that the SPD reports are generally trustworthy—even the Gestapo attested to their veracity—and the Nazi police reports perhaps somewhat less so. Cf. David Bankier, *The Germans and the Final Solution: Public Opinion Under Nazism* (Oxford, 1992), 7–9, 100–1; Gordon, *Hitler, Germans, and the "Jewish Question,"* 166–7, 209; Kershaw, *Popular Opinion and Political Dissent in the Third Reich,* 362; Kershaw, *The "Hitler Myth,"* 6–8.

conviction, the social segregation of the Jews. Yet in this respect, the Germans' "radical . . . treatment"—as Goldhagen puts it (*HWE:* 422)—of the Jews barely differed from the Jim Crow system in the American South.[44]

---

44. Bankier, *The Germans and the Final Solutions,* 69–73, 81–4 passim, 172 n68; Friedländer, *Nazi Germany and the Jews,* 22, 125–30, 232–6, 259, 323–4; Gellately, *The Gestapo and German Society,* 105 (quote), 106, 171; Gordon, *Hitler, Germans, and the "Jewish Question,"* 169, 171, 175, 206–8; Kater, "Everyday Anti-Semitism in Prewar Nazi Germany," 147–8, 154–6; Kershaw, *Popular Opinion and Political Dissent in the Third Reich,* 232, 233, 240, 243, 244, 256, 272–4; Kershaw, *The "Hitler Myth,"* 229–30; Otto Dov Kulka and Aron Rodrigue, "The German Population and the Jews in the Third Reich," in *Yad Vashem Studies,* XVI (Jerusalem, 1984), 426; Pulzer, *Jews and the German State,* 347; Reichmann, *Hostages of Civilization,* 233–4; Marlis Steinert, *Hitler's War and the Germans* (Athens, OH, 1977), 37, 40. Recall in this regard the following exchange between a British prosecutor and Hermann Göring at the Nuremberg Trials after World War II:

Q. Then, Dr. Göbbels raised the question of Jews travelling in railway trains?
A. Yes.
Q. Let me know if I quote correctly the dialogue between you and Dr. Göbbels on that subject. Dr. Göbbels said, "Furthermore, I advocate that Jews be banned from all public places where they might cause provocation. It is still possible for a Jew to share a sleeper with a German. Therefore, the Reich Ministry of Transport must issue a decree ordering that there shall be separate compartments for Jews. If this compartment is full, then the Jews cannot claim a seat. They can only occupy separate compartments after all Germans have secured seats. They must not mix with the Germans; if there is no more room, they will have to stand in the corridor." Is that right?
A. Yes, that is correct.
Q. Göring: "I think it would be more sensible to give them separate compartments." Göbbels: "Not if the train is overcrowded." Göring: "Just a moment. There will be only one Jewish coach. If that is filled up the other Jews will have to stay at home." Göbbels: "But suppose there are not many Jews going on the long-distance express train to Munich. Suppose there are two Jews on the train and the other compartments are overcrowded; these two Jews would then have a compartment to themselves. Therefore, the decree must state, Jews may claim a seat only after all Germans have secured a seat." Göring: "I would give the Jews one coach, or one compartment, and should a case such as you mentioned arise, and the train be overcrowded, believe me, we will not need a law. They will be kicked out all right, and will have to sit alone in the toilet all the way." Is that correct?
A. Yes. I was getting irritated when Göbbels came with his small details when important laws were being discussed. . . .
Q. Then Göbbels, who felt very strongly about these things, said that Jews should stand in the corridor, and you said that they would have to sit in the toilet. That is the way you said it? . . . (*The Trial of German Major War Criminals: Proceedings of the International Military Tribunal Sitting at Germany* [London, 1947], part 9, 258–9)

Consider the Nuremberg Laws. Repeatedly pointing to these enactments as the crystallization of the murderous Nazi mind-set, Goldhagen, for instance, writes:

> The eliminationist program had received at once its most coherent statement and its most powerful push forward. The Nuremberg Laws promised to accomplish what had heretofore for decades been but discussed and urged on ad nauseam. With this codifying moment of the Nazi German "religion," the regime held up the eliminationist writing on the Nazi tablets for every German to read. (*HWE:* 98; cf. 138)

The Nuremberg legislation stripped Jews of the franchise ("Reich Citizenship Law") and prohibited sexual relations between Jews and Germans ("The Law for the Protection of German Blood and Honor"). Yet, black people in the American South suffered from identical disabilities. Indeed, they did not effectively secure the vote, and the Supreme Court did not outlaw the antimiscegenation statutes, until the mid-1960s. These proscriptions enjoyed overwhelming support among Southern whites. Does that mean that nearly all

---

With his American colleagues standing by, the British prosecutor prudently focused on Göring's crudity and not—what is plainly the core moral outrage—the segregation law itself. Note also that the Reich did not enact legislation segregating public facilities until after Kristallnacht in November 1938. Pointing up the extremes of Nazi segregation policies, Saul Friedländer expresses near astonishment that, for example, "the benches actually carried the sign FOR ARYANS ONLY" (*Nazi Germany and the Jews,* 282, 388 n45). Yet such designations were a commonplace in the American South until the 1960s. In this connection, consider also Otto Dov Kulka's thesis that "the world historical-uniqueness of the Third Reich . . . lies precisely in the *duality*" of normal modernization, on the one hand, and enslavement and extermination of those excluded from the "national community," on the other ("Singularity and Its Relativization," in *Yad Vashem Studies,* XIX [Jerusalem, 1988], 169, emphasis in original). This same "duality," however, structured U.S. history in the formative nineteenth century.

Southern whites were genocidal racists waiting for a Hitler to "unleash" them?[45]

The German disposition to anti-Semitic violence is plainly the crucial test of Goldhagen's thesis. Seizing power, Hitler effectively opened the sluice gates. Moral and legal restraints were lifted. The opposition was crushed. Virulent anti-Semitic incitement was literally in the air. "The state," as Goldhagen puts it, "had implicitly declared the Jews to be 'fair game'— beings who were to be eliminated from German society, by whatever means necessary, including violence" (HWE: 95).[46] What did the German people do? Did they spontaneously indulge in anti-Semitic pogroms? Did they join in the Nazi pogroms? Did they approve the Nazi pogroms? Did they, at bare minimum, condone the Nazi pogroms? The voluminous scholarly evidence points to a uniform, unequivocal answer to all these questions: No. There were few if any popular German assaults on the Jews. Indeed, Germans overwhelmingly condemned the Nazi anti-Semitic atrocities.

For "far greater empirical support for my positions than space permits me to offer here," Goldhagen advises, readers should consult David Bankier's study *The Germans and the Final Solution: Public Opinion Under Nazism* (HWE: 497–8 n24).

---

45. For the Nuremberg Laws, cf. Helmut Krausnick, "The Persecution of the Jews," in Helmut Krausnick et al., *Anatomy of the SS State* (New York, 1965), 32–3, and Mommsen, "The Realization of the Unthinkable," 103–5. For popular German reaction to the Nuremberg Laws, cf. esp. Otto Dov Kulka, " 'Public Opinion' in Nazi Germany and the 'Jewish Question,' " in *The Jerusalem Quarterly*, Fall 1982, 124–35. Kulka concludes that most Germans supported the laws, although a "quite sizeable portion of the population was indifferent" (135). The U.S. Voting Rights Act was passed in 1965. The Supreme Court first declared a state miscegenation law unconstitutional in 1967 (*Loving v. Virginia*).

46. Directly contradicting himself, Goldhagen writes elsewhere that "Germans' profound hatred of Jews . . . had in the 1930s *by necessity* lain relatively dormant" (HWE: 449, my emphasis).

Consider then Bankier's conclusions. During the first years of Nazi anti-Semitic incitement, most Germans ("large sectors," "the bulk," "sizable parts") found "the form of persecution abhorrent," expressed "misgivings about the brutal methods employed," "remained on the sidelines," "severely condemned the persecution," etc. With the revival of Nazi anti-Semitic terror in 1935, "large sections of the population were repelled by the Sturmer methods and refused to comply with demands to take action against the Jews." Indeed, the "vast majority of the population approved the Nuremberg Laws" not only because they "identified with the racialist policy" but "especially" because "a permanent framework of discrimination had been created that would end the reign of terror and set precise limits to antisemitic activities." "Sturmer methods and the violence" in the years 1936–7 "met with the same disapproval as in the past." "The overwhelming majority approved social segregation and economic destruction of the Jews" on the eve of Kristallnacht in 1938 "but not outbursts of brute force. . . . [I]t was not Jew-hatred in the Nazi sense." "All sections of the population," Bankier reports, "reacted with shock" to Kristallnacht. "There were few occasions, if any, in the Third Reich," Kershaw similarly recalls, "which produced such a widespread wave of revulsion," reaching "deep into the ranks" of the Nazi party itself. The motives behind these outpourings of popular disgust, to be sure, were not unalloyed. Some Germans evinced genuine moral outrage. Some recoiled from the sheer brutality of the violence (which also defaced Germany's image). Some opposed the destruction only because it squandered material resources. Yet, whatever the motive, Goldhagen's thesis is unsustainable.[47]

---

47. Bankier, *The Germans and the Final Solution,* chap. 4; Kershaw, *Popular Opinion and Political Dissent in the Third Reich,* 271, 265 (cf. 172, 234–5, 239, 240,

For argument's sake, let us assume the worst-case scenario: Germans repudiated Nazi anti-Semitic violence not on strictly humanitarian grounds but, rather, because it was gratuitously cruel and economically wasteful. According to Goldhagen, however, these were precisely the differentiae of the Nazi genocide. The "limitless cruelty" of the German perpetrators, Goldhagen emphasizes, was "a constituent feature of the Holocaust, as central to it as the killing itself" (*Reply:* 38; I will return to this crucial distinction in part 2). Goldhagen also devotes a very significant part of his study (281–323) to demonstrating that, in the hierarchy of "guiding values" in the German "work" camps, persecution of the Jews always took precedence over "economic rationality" (*HWE:* 322). Regardless of the reason, then, the German people's overwhelming condemnation of Nazi anti-Semitic violence is conclusive evidence that Goldhagen's "monocausal explanation" is false. Note further that, according to Goldhagen, a crucial facet of the Nazi genocide was the voluntarism of the perpetrators. Always taking the initiative, ordinary Germans—to quote a typical passage—"easily and with alacrity became exe-

---

243–4, 256, 260–74). For further documentation of Bankier's conclusions, cf. also Friedländer, *Nazi Germany and the Jews,* 125, 163–4, 294–5; Gordon, *Hitler, Germans and the "Jewish Question,"* 159, 173, 175–80, 206–8, 265–7; Ian Kershaw, "German Popular Opinion and the 'Jewish Question,' 1939–1943: Some Further Reflections," in Arnold Paucker (ed.), *The Jews in Nazi Germany, 1933–1943* (Tübingen, 1986), 368–9; Kershaw, *The "Hitler Myth,"* 229–30, 235–7; Kulka, " 'Public Opinion' in Nazi Germany and the 'Jewish Question,' " 138–44; Kulka and Rodrigue, "The German Population and the Jews in the Third Reich," 432; Mommsen, "The Realization of the Unthinkable," 116; Franz Neumann, *Behemoth* (New York, 1942), 121; Pulzer, *Jews and the German State,* 347; Pulzer, *The Rise of Political Anti-Semitism in Germany and Austria,* 71; Reichmann, *Hostages of Civilization,* 201, 233–4, 238; Steinert, *Hitler's War and the Germans,* 37, 40; Herbert A. Strauss, "Jewish Emigration from Germany—Nazi Policies and Jewish Responses," in Leo Baeck Institute, *Year Book XXV* (New York, 1980), 331. Bankier discounts while Kershaw credits German moral outrage to Kristallnacht. Kulka and Rodrigue reasonably conclude that "we shall probably never know what the true proportions of both attitudes were."

cutioners of Jews" (*HWE:* 395; I will return to this point as well in part 2). Yet as we have seen, spontaneous German anti-Semitic attacks rarely occurred. On the eve of the Nazi holocaust, the German people were, on Goldhagen's own terms, very far from "Nazified." Indeed, there was much less popular participation in and support for violent racist incitement in Nazi Germany than in the American South.[48]

Apparently aware that the crushing weight of scholarly evidence obliterates his thesis, Goldhagen improvises a three-prong damage control strategy: tacit admission, minimization, and misrepresentation. Given space limitations, I can only sample his procedures here.

---

48. The scholarly consensus is that "[a]lthough without doubt some individual members of the white community condemned lynching, it is equally clear that a majority supported outlaw mob violence" (Stewart E. Tolnay and E. M. Beck, *A Festival of Violence: An Analysis of Southern Lynchings, 1882–1930* [Chicago, 1992], 28; cf. Neil R. McMillen, *Dark Journey* [Chicago, 1989], chap. 7, esp. 238ff., and Arthur F. Raper, *The Tragedy of Lynching* [New York, 1969], 47). Between 1890 and 1930, fully three thousand black people were lynched. One may add that, for sheer brutality, Southern violence was in a class apart. Consider this description from the *New York Tribune* of a turn-of-the-century Georgia lynching:

Sam Hose . . . was burned at the stake in a public road, one and a half miles from here. Before the torch was applied to the pyre, the Negro was deprived of his ears, fingers and other portions of his body with surprising fortitude. Before the body was cool, it was cut into pieces, the bones were crushed into small bits and even the tree upon which the wretch met his fate was torn up and disposed of as souvenirs. The Negro's heart was cut into several pieces, as was also his liver. Those unable to obtain ghastly relics directly, paid more fortunate possessors extravagant sums for them. Small pieces of bone went for 25 cents and a bit of liver, crisply cooked, for 10 cents. (Tolnay and Beck, 23)

Such grisly scenes were inconceivable in prewar Nazi Germany.

TACIT ADMISSION	MINIMIZATION	MISREPRESENTATION
Goldhagen acknowledges the evidence but not its devastating implications for his thesis. For example:	Goldhagen acknowledges the evidence but denies that it undermines his thesis. For example:	Goldhagen mangles the evidence. For example:
"The law excluding Jews from the civil service, being unaccompanied by public displays of brutality, was, not surprisingly, widely popular in Germany" (*HWE*: 91).	"The criticism of *Kristallnacht*'s licentious violence and wasteful destruction that could be heard around Germany should be understood as the limited criticism of an eliminationist path that the overwhelming majority of Germans considered to be fundamentally sound, but which, in this case, had taken a momentary wrong turn" (*HWE*: 102; cf. 101, 103, 120–1, 123). (Weren't "licentious violence" and "wasteful destruction" the hallmarks of the Nazi genocide?)	Recalling inter alia the "[p]hysical and increased verbal attacks upon Jews, both spontaneous ones from ordinary Germans and ones orchestrated by government and party institutions," Goldhagen adds: "the vast majority of the German people . . . were aware of what their government and their countrymen were doing to the Jews, assented to the measures, and, when the opportunity presented itself, lent their active support to them" (*HWE*: 89–90). (Didn't Goldhagen's main empirical source state that Germans overwhelmingly opposed Nazi violence?)

(Continued)

TACIT ADMISSION	MINIMIZATION	MISREPRESENTATION
Recalling the "uncoordinated and often wild attacks upon Jews" during the first years of Nazi rule, Goldhagen observes that "many Germans" felt "unsettled" (*HWE*: 97).	"[E]pisodic distemper with aspects of the regime's assault on the Jews should not be understood as being indicative of a widespread, general rejection of the eliminationist ideal and program. . . . [T]he character and overwhelming plenitude of the counter-evidence . . . is vastly greater than Germans' numerically paltry expressions of disapproval of what . . . can be seen to have been generally only *specific aspects* of the larger eliminationist program—and not its governing principles" (*HWE*: 120, emphasis in original; cf. 91).	"The attacks upon Jews during these first years of Nazi governance of Germany were so widespread—and broad-based—that it would be grievously wrong to attribute them solely to the toughs of the SA, as if the wider German public had no influence over, or part in, the violence" (*HWE*: 95).

TACIT ADMISSION	MINIMIZATION	MISREPRESENTATION
(Continued)		
"The reaction of the populace at large" to Nazi initiatives "was one of general approval . . . , though it was accompanied by significant disapproval of the licentious brutality" (HWE: 99).	Conceding that "[o]rdinary Germans did not leap to mass extermination on their own, or generally even urge it," Goldhagen explains that "Hitler was already working towards this goal with heart and soul, so many Germans sat by, satisfied that their government was doing the best that any government conceivably could" (HWE: 445–6). (Weren't Germans anxiously awaiting a Hitler to "unleash" and "unshackle" their "pent-up antisemitic passion"? Seizing every opportunity, didn't Germans leap "with alacrity" to kill Jews during the Nazi genocide?)	"In light of the widespread persecution and violence that occurred throughout . . . Germany, Kristallnacht was, in one sense, but the crowning moment in the wild domestic terror that Germans perpetrated upon Jews" (HWE: 99; cf. 100–1).
To document that "workers . . . were, on the issue of the Jews, in general accord with the Nazis," Goldhagen cites an SPD report stating that "[t]he general antisemitic psychosis affects . . . our comrades" but "[a]ll are decided opponents of violence" (HWE: 106–7).	"No evidence suggests that any but an insignificant scattering of Germans harbored opposition to the eliminationist program save for its most brutally wanton aspects" (HWE: 438–9; cf. 509–10 n165).	"The perpetrators [of the Nazi genocide], from Hitler to the lowliest officials, were openly proud of their actions, of their achievements; during the 1930s, they proclaimed and carried them out in full view and with the general approval of the Volk" (HWE: 429; cf. 430).

Left without a shred of scholarly evidence that Germans overwhelmingly savored the prospect of massacring Jewry, Goldhagen devises more ingenious methods of proof. Thus, to document the "whiff of genocide" in the "antisemitic German atmosphere," Goldhagen quotes an American journalist's murderous conversations with "Nazi circles" and "at a luncheon or dinner with Nazis" (*HWE:* 595 n68). "It is oxymoronic," according to Goldhagen, "to suggest that those who stood with curiosity gazing upon the annihilative inferno of *Kristallnacht*" did not relish the violence and destruction. Apparently never having witnessed a crowd mill about a burning edifice, Goldhagen writes: "People generally flee scenes and events that they consider to be horrific, criminal, or dangerous" (*HWE:* 440).

Although there was no palpable evidence in the 1930s of Americans' intent to kill Japanese, Goldhagen finally analogizes, they did so "willingly . . . and fully believing in the justice of their cause" during World War II (*HWE:* 446). The comparison is instructive. The merciless war in the Pacific, John Dower has argued, was the culmination of a plurality of factors: pervasive anti-Asian prejudice, furor over the Pearl Harbor attack, inflammatory war propaganda, brutalizing combat, and so on.[49] To reckon by Goldhagen's analogy, however, the explanation is rather more simple: Americans were homicidal racists.

Even during the early war years, most Germans repudiated Nazi anti-Semitism. In September 1941 the Nazis issued a decree forcing Jews to wear the yellow star. "A negative reac-

49. John W. Dower, *War Without Mercy* (New York, 1986).

tion to the labelling," Bankier reports, was the "more typical public response." Indeed "people were often demonstratively kind," according to reliable accounts. "Many displayed forms of disobedience, offering Jews cigars and cigarettes, giving children sweets, or standing up for Jews on trams and underground trains." "Germans clearly could not tolerate," Bankier infers, "actions which outraged their sense of decency, even towards stigmatized Jews." Shocked and appalled by such dissent, the Nazis intensified anti-Jewish propaganda and even enacted a new law sanctioning philo-Semitic displays with three months' internment in a concentration camp.[50] Although listing Bankier's study as his main empirical source, Goldhagen omits altogether these remarkable findings. Rather he reports:

> Wearing such a visible target among such a hostile populace . . . caused Jews to feel acute insecurity, and, because any German passerby could now identify them easily, Jews, especially Jewish children, suffered increased verbal and physical assaults. . . . The introduction of the yellow star also meant that all Germans could now better recognize, monitor, and shun those bearing the mark of the social dead. (*HWE:* 138–9)

With the passage of time and especially as the war took a more disastrous turn, Germans grew increasingly insensitive to Jewish suffering. Propaganda played a part, as did the escalating repression and physical isolation of the Jews. Then the callousness toward human life typically attending war—exacerbated by the terror bombing and worsening deprivations on the home front—set in. Turning ever more inward, Germans

---

50. Bankier, *The Germans and the Final Solution,* 124–30.

focused on the exigencies of survival. Hardened and bitter, in search of a scapegoat, they occasionally lashed out at the weak.[51] To illustrate this gradual coarsening of heart, Bankier first recalls "not unusual" episodes in 1941 when, breaking the law and outraging Nazi authorities, Germans surrendered their streetcar seats to aged Jews, eliciting "the general approval of the other passengers." Yet by 1942, according to Bankier, Germans displaying sympathy for Jews were hooted in public. He recounts a particularly brutal incident also on a streetcar. Citing *only* this last episode in his book, Goldhagen goes on to criticize Bankier's balanced conclusion based on *all* the evidence:

> It is difficult to understand why Bankier . . . concludes that "incidents of this sort substantiate the contention that day-to-day contact with a virulent, antisemitic atmosphere progressively dulled people's sensitivity to the plight of their Jewish neighbors." . . . That any but a small number of Germans ever possessed "sensitivity to the plight of their Jewish neighbors" during the Nazi period is an assumption which cannot be substantiated, and which . . . is undermined by the empirical evidence which Bankier presents throughout his book. (*HWE:* 105, 502 n90)

Truly, the Germans' progressively dulled sensitivities are "an assumption which cannot be substantiated"—if all the empirical substantiation is subject to excision.

Although unaware of the full scope of the Judeocide, most Germans did know, or could have known if they chose to, that

---

51. Kershaw, *Popular Opinion and Political Dissent in the Third Reich,* chap. 9 passim; Steinert, *Hitler's War and the Germans,* 136–45, 334–5.

massive atrocities were being committed in the East. There is no evidence, however, that most Germans approved these murderous acts. Indeed, precisely because Hitler knew he could not count on enthusiastic popular support, the Final Solution was shrouded in secrecy and all public discussion of Jewry's fate was banned.[52] The near consensus in the scholarly literature is that most Germans looked on with malignant indifference. Ian Kershaw, who has written most authoritatively on this topic, summarizes:

> Apathy and "moral indifference" to the treatment and fate of the Jews was the most widespread attitude of all. This was not a neutral stance. It was a deliberate turning away from any personal responsibility, acceptance of the state's right to decide on an issue of little personal concern to most Germans . . . , the shying away from anything which might produce trouble or danger. This apathy was compatible with a number of internalised attitudes towards Jews, not least with passive or latent anti-Semitism—the feeling that there *was* a "Jewish Question" and that something needed to be done about it. (emphasis in original)

It bears emphasis that Germany's anti-Semitic legacy did constitute a vital precondition for the genocide. Had Jews not been placed outside the community of moral concern, Kershaw underlines, the Nazis could not have committed their monstrous deeds:

---

52. Bankier, *The Germans and the Final Solution,* chap. 8; Gordon, *Hitler, Germans, and the "Jewish Question,"* 182–6; Hans Mommsen, "What Did the Germans Know About the Genocide of the Jews?" in Walter H. Pehle (ed.), *November 1938* (New York, 1991); Mommsen, "The Realization of the Unthinkable," 108, 128, 131 n12; Steinert, *Hitler's War and the Germans,* 55, 140–5 passim, 335. Probably only a minority of Germans had specific knowledge of the death camps or gassings.

> The lack of interest in or exclusion of concern for the fate
> of racial, ethnic, or religious minority groups marks . . .
> at the societal level a significant prerequisite for the geno-
> cidal process, allowing the momentum created by the
> fanatical hatred of a section of the population to gather
> force, especially, of course, when supported by the power
> of the state.

This is a far cry, however, from asserting that ordinary German anti-Semitism—let alone ordinary German anti-Semitism before Hitler's reign—in itself accounts for the Nazi genocide.

Indeed, Kershaw suggests that little in the German response was "peculiarly German or specific only to the 'Jewish Question,' " and, conversely, that most peoples similarly situated would probably not have responded in more "honorable" fashion than the Germans.[53] Vehemently dissenting, Goldhagen maintains that such alleged indifference in the face of mass slaughter is a "virtual psychological impossibility" (*HWE*: 439–41).[54] Yet how differently did ordinary Americans react to the slaughter of four million Indochinese, ordinary French to the slaughter of one million Algerians, or, for that matter, ordinary non-Germans to the slaughter of the Jews?

---

53. Kershaw, "German Popular Opinion and the 'Jewish Question,' 1939–1943: Some Further Reflections," 366–84 (quote at 383–4); Ian Kershaw, "German Public Opinion During the Final Solution: Information, Comprehension, Reactions," in Asher Cohen et al., *Comprehending the Holocaust* (New York, 1988), 146–55 (quotes at 146–7, 155).

54. In his famous exchange with Martin Broszat, Saul Friedländer maintained in a similar vein that "normal life with the knowledge of ongoing massive crimes committed by one's own nation and one's own society is not so normal after all" ("A Controversy About the Historicization of National Socialism," in *Reworking the Past,* 120, cf. 131).

2

Perpetrating the Genocide

When the correlations are made of the Germans' anti-Jewish measures with their deduced or imputed intentions, Hitler's hypothesized psychological states and moods, and the Germans' military fortune, the correlation that stands out, that jumps out, as having been more significant than any other (than all of the others) is that Hitler opted for genocide at the first moment that the policy became practical.

HITLER'S WILLING EXECUTIONERS, 161

With the onset of the Nazi holocaust, the validity of Goldhagen's thesis ceases to be at issue. On the one hand, all evidence points to the conclusion that, on the eve of the genocide, the vast majority of Germans were *not* in thrall to a homicidal malice toward Jewry. On the other hand, it is simply not possible, after 1941, to isolate, among the sundry factors potentially spurring German behavior—an anti-Semitic legacy, virulent Nazi propaganda, brutalization of war, etc.—a "monocausal explanation" of the Judeocide.[55] Thus, even if

---

55. For the corrosive effects of the brutalizing combat and Nazi propaganda on ordinary German perpetrators, cf. esp. Omer Bartov's companion studies, *The Eastern Front, 1941–45* (New York, 1986) and *Hitler's Army* (Oxford, 1991).

everything Goldhagen maintains about the Nazi holocaust is
accurate, his thesis remains false or at best moot. Goldhagen's
rendering, however, is *not* accurate. Indeed, in a veritable negative tour de force, Goldhagen manages to get nearly everything about the Nazi holocaust wrong. The wrong questions
are posed. The wrong answers are given. The wrong lessons are
learned.

V.

Crediting himself as being the first to reckon the magnitude
of German complicity in the Nazi holocaust, Goldhagen
boasts:

> Until now no one else has discussed seriously the number
> of people who perpetrated the genocide. . . . The critics

Goldhagen denies that the war brutalized Germans: "The 'brutalization' that the
men underwent during the fighting had no appreciable effect on their treatment
of Jews. Similarly none of the evidence suggests that prolonged engagement in
genocidal slaughter altered the treatment that the men of police battalions meted
out to Jews" (*HWE:* 275). Yet he also reports, e.g., that a police battalion lieu-
tenant who originally "refused to allow his men to participate in the killing of
the Jews . . . was later to become a zealous killer, who performed with extreme
ardor and brutality towards the victims" (*HWE:* 535 n4). Goldhagen does not
account for this metamorphosis. Is "brutalization" so implausible an explanation? Goldhagen also dismisses as "nonsense" the postwar rationale of, e.g., the
police battalion members that their participation in the genocide was partly in
reaction to Allied atrocities: "Their killing began when Germany reigned
supreme and hardly a bomb was being dropped on it" (*HWE:* 537 n23). Police
Battalion 101 (the focus of Goldhagen's study) embarked on outright genocide in
July 1942. Yet Britain launched the first bomber offensive deliberately aimed at
civilian German targets in May 1940. By early 1942, it was engaged in massive
terror-bombing of German cities. The Allies, incidentally, inflicted far more
civilian casualties on Germany than they suffered from the Germans. Almost
entirely restricted to Britain, German bombing of civilians caused about 51,000
deaths. The Allied air assaults, however, left about 600,000 German civilians
dead (cf. Clive Ponting, *Armageddon* [New York, 1995], 239–40).

do not bother to inform their readers that I am the first to discuss the numbers (and the problems of providing an estimate), let alone to convey to readers the significance of the findings or of the fact that we have had to wait until 1996 to learn one of the most elementary facts about the Holocaust. (*Reply:* 42)

Yet consider Goldhagen's calculations (*HWE:* 166–7). He first estimates that, if all German perpetrators, direct and indirect, of the genocide are included, the number "ran into the millions." He next estimates that "the number of people who were actual perpetrators was also enormous" and "might run into the millions." He then qualifies, however, that "the number who became perpetrators of the Holocaust (in the sense that it is meant here) was certainly over one hundred thousand" and perhaps as many as "five hundred thousand or more." But what is "the sense that it is meant here," if not direct and indirect perpetrators combined or direct perpetrators alone? Compounding the confusion, Goldhagen earlier explicitly defines a perpetrator for the purposes of his study as any direct or indirect participant in the genocide.[56] This pre-

---

56. "A perpetrator is anyone who knowingly contributed in some intimate way to the mass slaughter of Jews, generally anyone who worked in an institution of genocidal killing. This includes all people who themselves took the lives of Jews, and all those who set the scene for the final lethal act, whose help was instrumental in bringing about the deaths of Jews. So anyone who shot Jews as part of a killing squad was a perpetrator. Those who rounded up these same Jews, deported them (with knowledge of their fate) to a killing location, or cordoned off the area where their compatriots shot them were also perpetrators, even if they themselves did not do the actual killing. Perpetrators include railroad engineers and administrators who knew that they were transporting Jews to their deaths. They include any Church officials who knew that their participation in the identification of Jews as non-Christians would lead to the deaths of the Jews. They include the by now proverbial 'desk-murderer' . . . who himself may not have seen the victims yet whose paperwork lubricated the wheels of deportation and destruction" (*HWE:* 164; cf. 165, 523 n3).

sumably being "the sense that it is meant here," the total number of direct and indirect German perpetrators thus runs *not* into the millions but at most the hundreds of thousands. What is more, Goldhagen acknowledges in an endnote that all his calculations are pure guesswork: "Early in my research, I decided that deriving a good estimate of the number of people who were perpetrators would consume more time than I could profitably devote to it, given my other research objectives. Still, I am confident in asserting that the number was huge" (*HWE:* 525 n13). Indeed, even this last asseveration is plainly untrue. The estimate for perpetrators Goldhagen most often cites is one hundred thousand. Even assuming for argument's sake that it includes only direct participants, this figure is still not at all "huge." Goldhagen seems unaware that his research is significant only if—as Hilberg suggests—the perpetrators of the genocide were *qualitatively* representative of German society generally. Goldhagen's *quantitative* finding is comparatively trivial. To be sure, according to Goldhagen's idiosyncratic bookkeeping, one hundred thousand perpetrators from the German population of eighty million at the time proves that "most of the people . . . had done many criminal things."[57]

Based mainly on the archives of postwar investigations and trials, the core of Goldhagen's study is an analysis of the German police battalions.[58] Following Christopher Browning, Goldhagen maintains that these "agents of genocide" were more or less typical Germans. Also like Browning, Goldhagen reports that the police battalions were often not obliged to kill

---

57. Transcript, *Dateline NBC,* 28 March 1997.
58. For Goldhagen's misrepresentation of the German archives, cf. Ruth Bettina Birn's essay in this volume.

Jews. Explicitly given the option of not participating, the overwhelming majority chose not to exercise it. Indeed, those who opted out suffered no real penalties (*HWE:* 181–5, 203–22 passim).[59] In their testimony, the police battalions didn't at all acknowledge anti-Semitism as a motivating factor. Making a persuasive case that the near-total silence on Jews was partly disingenuous, Browning nonetheless flatly denies that virulent, Nazi-like anti-Semitism was the prime impetus behind the police battalions' implementation of the Final Solution.[60] To sustain his contrary thesis, Goldhagen focuses on the gratuitous cruelty attending the genocide. The argument he makes comprises two interrelated but also distinct propositions: (1) the police battalions implemented the Final Solution with gratuitous cruelty, and (2) gratuitous cruelty is the hallmark of virulent, Nazi-like anti-Semitism. I will address these propositions in reverse order.

"Not only the killing but also *how* the Germans killed must be explained," according to Goldhagen. "The 'how' frequently provides great insight into the 'why.' " It is Goldhagen's main theoretical contention that the propensity for "gratuitous cruelty, such as beating, mocking, torturing Jews"—a cruelty

---

59. Christopher Browning, *Ordinary Men* (New York, 1992), 45–8, 61ff., 170–1. Even Nazi regime stalwarts organized in, e.g., the Einsatzgruppen, could refuse participation in the Judeocide without suffering substantive penalties. Indeed, all German perpetrators could also exercise many options short of outright refusal to evade murderous orders. On these points, cf. Hans Buchheim, "Command and Compliance," in Helmut Krausnick, Hans Buchheim, Martin Broszat, Hans-Adolf Jacobsen, *Anatomy of the SS State* (New York, 1965), 373–5, 387; Hilberg, *Perpetrators, Victims, Bystanders,* 55; Hilberg, *The Destruction of the European Jews,* vol. 3, 1024–5; Heinz Höhne, *The Order of the Death's Head* (London, 1969), 357; Ernst Klee, Willi Dressen, Volker Riess (eds.), *"The Good Old Days"* (New York, 1991), xx, 62, 75–86.
60. Browning, *Ordinary Men,* 73, 150ff, 184.

"which had no instrumental, pragmatic purpose save the satisfaction and pleasure of the perpetrators"—was the hallmark
of the "Nazified German mind" in thrall to "demonological
antisemitism." Contrariwise, had they not been Nazi-like
anti-Semites, the German perpetrators would have been "cold,
mechanical executioners," "emotionless or reluctant functionaries," etc. (*HWE:* 17, 188, 228, 256, 259, 386, 388–9,
396–8, 400, 457, 480 n40, emphasis in original).[61]
The remarkable thing about Goldhagen's argument is that
the exact opposite is true. What distinguished Nazi anti-
Semitism *was* the reluctant and mechanical as against the gratuitously cruel implementation of the Final Solution. "The
killing of the Jews," reports Raul Hilberg, "was regarded as
historical necessity."

> The soldier had to "understand" this. If for any reason he
> was instructed to help the SS and Police in their task, he
> was expected to obey orders. However, if he killed a Jew
> spontaneously, voluntarily, or without instruction,
> merely because he *wanted* to kill, then he committed
> an abnormal act, worthy perhaps of an "Eastern Euro-
> pean." . . . Herein lay the crucial difference between the
> man who "overcame" himself to kill and one who wan-
> tonly committed atrocities. The former was regarded as a
> good soldier and a true Nazi; the latter was a person with-
> out self-control. . . . (emphasis in original)

Addressing the Nazi fighting elite, SS leader Heinrich
Himmler accordingly avowed that the Final Solution had
become "the most painful question of my life"; that he "hated

---

61. Faulting "conventional explanations" for ignoring the cruelty dimension,
Goldhagen, in his inimitable style, alleges: "They do not acknowledge the 'inhu-
manity' of the deeds as being anything other than epiphenomenal to the under-
lying phenomenon to be explained" (*HWE:* 392).

this bloody business" that had disturbed him to the "depth" of his "soul," but everyone must do his duty, "however hard it might be"; that "we have completed this painful task out of love for our people"; that it was "the curse of the great to have to walk over corpses"; that "we have been called upon to fulfill a repulsive duty," and he "would not like it if Germans did such a thing gladly"; that "an execution is a grim duty for our men" and "if we had not felt it to be hideous and frightful, we should not have been Germans," but nevertheless "we must grit our teeth and do our duty," etc.

In his perversely sanctimonious postwar memoir, *Commandant of Auschwitz* (generally accepted by scholars as representing honest, if barbaric, sentiments), the exemplary ultra-Nazi Rudolf Hoess similarly recalled being "deeply marked" and "tormented" by the "mass extermination, with all the attendant circumstances" of this "monstrous 'work.'" Regarding the "Extermination Order" for the Gypsies—"my best-loved prisoners, if I may put it that way"—Hoess reflects: "Nothing surely is harder than to grit one's teeth and go through with such a thing, coldly, pitilessly and without mercy." To implement the Final Solution, "I had to exercise intense self-control in order to prevent my innermost doubts and feelings of oppression from becoming apparent. . . . My pity was so great that I longed to vanish from the scene. . . ."

Loathsome undertaking that it was, the Judeocide was supposed to be executed with stoicism. "Sadism," reports Heinz Höhne, "was only one facet of mass extermination and one disapproved of by SS Headquarters." Repudiating "crude" anti-Semitism, the Nazi elite sought to "solve the so-called Jewish problem in a cold, rational manner." "The new type of man of violence," Joachim Fest likewise observes, "was concerned with the dispassionate extermination of real or possible oppo-

nents, not with the primitive release of sadistic impulses."
This ideal Nazi rejection of compulsive in favor of calculated
violence, Hans Mommsen emphasizes, was "fundamental to
the entire system." It did not at all, to be sure, spring from
humanitarian impulses. Rather, gratuitous cruelty was seen as
beneath the moral dignity and undermining the combat discipline of the German executioners.

Rejecting "from inner conviction" the "Bolshevist method
of physical extermination of a people as un-Germanic," SS
leader Heinrich Himmler resolved to implement the Final
Solution "cooly and clearly; even while obeying the official
order to commit murder, the SS man must remain 'decent' "
(Höhne). "We shall never be rough or heartless where it is not
necessary; that is clear," Himmler admonished. "Be hard but
do not become hardened" and "intervene at once" should "a
Commander exceed his duty or show signs that his sense of
restraint is becoming blurred." Regarding unauthorized
assaults on Jews, Himmler's legal staff accordingly instructed
that, if the motive was "purely political, there should be no
punishment unless such is necessary for the maintenance of
discipline. . . . If the motive is selfish, sadistic or sexual, judi-
cial punishment should be imposed for murder or manslaugh-
ter as the case may be." Thus, in one notorious SS and Police
Supreme Court verdict, an SS officer was convicted not for the
actual murder of Jews but inter alia for the "vicious excesses,"
"Bolshevik methods," "vicious brutality," "cruel actions," etc.
that attended the murders. (Goldhagen refers to this proceeding but not the conviction for gratuitous cruelty; *HWE:* 585
n73.) "Himmler, in short, was not a simple, bloodthirsty,
sadistic monster," concludes biographer Richard Breitman. "If
a sadist is one who delights in personally inflicting pain or
death on others, or in witnessing others inflict them, then

Himmler was not a sadist. . . . Himmler was the ultimate bureaucrat." The "horrors of the concentration camps," Hoess avows, did not receive his sanction. Evidently the Auschwitz commandant intends, not the systematic mass extermination overseen by him but, rather, the sadistic outbursts he purports to have "used every means at my disposal to stop." "I myself never maltreated a prisoner, far less killed one. Nor have I ever tolerated maltreatment by my subordinates." "I was never cruel." Repeatedly professing profound disgust at the "malignancy, wickedness and brutality" of SS guards who did gratuitously torture camp inmates, Hoess muses: "They did not regard prisoners as human beings at all. . . . They regarded the sight of corporal punishment being inflicted as an excellent spectacle, a kind of peasant merrymaking. I was certainly not one of these." The Kapos—prisoner-functionaries in charge of the work detachments—indulging orgies of violence aroused Hoess's deepest contempt: "They were soulless and had no feelings whatsoever. I find it incredible that human beings could ever turn into such beasts. . . . It was simply gruesome."[62] Indeed, former inmates of the Nazi concentration camps typically testify that the Kapos were, in the words of Auschwitz survivor Dr. Viktor E. Frankl, "harder on the prisoners than were the guards, and beat them more cruelly than

---

62. On these and related points, cf. Omer Bartov, *The Eastern Front, 1941–45,* 115; Richard Breitman, *The Architect of Genocide* (New York, 1991), 250; Buchheim, "Command and Compliance," 338 (quote), 351, 361–2, 363 (quote), 372; Joachim Fest, *The Face of the Third Reich* (New York, 1970), 115 (quote), 118 (quote), 121 (quote); Hilberg, *The Destruction of the European Jews,* vol. i, 326 (quote), 332–3 (quote), vol. iii, 904, 1009–10; Rudolf Hoess, *Commandant of Auschwitz* (London, 1974), 70, 142–3, 150, 171–3, 201–3; Höhne, *The Order of the Death's Head,* 307, 325 (quote), 328 (quote), 364–6, 382 (quote), 383, 386ff.; Klee et al., *"The Good Old Days,"* 195ff. (quote); Mommsen, "The Realization of the Unthinkable," 99.

the SS men did."[63] To reckon by Goldhagen's standard, not Hoess or Himmler but the Kapo underling was the quintessential "Nazified German mind" in thrall to "demonological antisemitism."

On the other hand, Goldhagen does, for example, mention that a senior SS official "who was no friend of the Jews"; *Das Schwarze Korps,* "the official organ of the SS, the most ideologically radical of all Nazi papers and naturally also a virulently antisemitic one"; and "even the commandant of Auschwitz, Rudolf Hoess, who presided over the mass murder of hundreds of thousands of Jews," repudiated, indeed were "repelled" by, the "unnecessary brutality," "frenzied sadists," "senseless acts of terror," etc. He doesn't, however, register the potentially fatal implications of these acknowledgments for his thesis (*HWE:* 105, 121, 394, 509–10 n165). Compounding error with contradiction, Goldhagen instead avers that the "Nazified German mind" was equally compatible with a broad spectrum of types—ranging from the "reveling, sadistic slayers" and the "zealous but faint-of-heart killers" to the "dedicated but non-celebratory executioners" and the "approving but uneasy and conflicted killers"—and that "it is hard to know what the distribution of the various types was" (*HWE:* 259–61; cf. 509–10 n165). That being the case, gratuitous cruelty plainly did *not* distinguish the "Nazified German mind." Goldhagen's fixation on the gratuitous cruelty of Germans is thus, even on his own terms, wrongheaded: the "sadistic slayer" is, for Goldhagen, no more proof of a "Nazified German mind" than the "uneasy and conflicted killer." Put otherwise, by Goldhagen's own admission, the

---

63. Viktor E. Frankl, *Man's Search for Meaning* (New York, 1984), 18, cf. 93; cf. also Wolfgang Sofsky, *The Order of Terror* (Princeton, NJ 1997), 137–49 passim.

"how" does not—contrary to his crucial thesis—"provide great insight into the 'why.' "

Consider now Goldhagen's complementary empirical claim. The gratuitous cruelty of the police battalions was pervasive. Goldhagen's study is mostly given over to chronicling German atrocities attendant on the Final Solution. Undaunted by the "horror, brutality, and frequently gruesomeness of the killing operations," the police battalions, according to Goldhagen, "easily became genocidal killers" of Jews. Indeed, Goldhagen maintains that the police battalions tortured and murdered Jews with "relish and excess," "cruel abandon," "unmistakable alacrity," "evident gusto," "dedication and zeal," as a "pleasurable pursuit," "in the most gratuitous, willful manner," etc. (*HWE*: 19, 185, 191, 237, 238, 255, 256, 259, 378, 387, 447). Goldhagen underlines that the police battalions committed their monstrous deeds openly (e.g., with "loved ones" in attendance), and even "memorialized" them in photographs: "It is as if they were saying, 'Here is a great event. Anyone who wants to preserve for himself images of the heroic accomplishments can order copies' " (*HWE*: 241–7).

First, a brief word about this latter argument. To prove that ordinary Germans were in thrall to homicidal anti-Semitism before Hitler's rise to power, Goldhagen points to the public aspect of the atrocities. Yet compare the war in the Pacific. Recalling that the Allied combatants' practice of collecting Japanese ears "was no secret," John Dower reports:

> "The other night," read an account in the Marine monthly *Leatherneck* in mid-1943, "Stanley emptied his pocket of 'souvenirs'—eleven ears from dead Japs. It was not disgusting, as it would be from the civilian point of view. None of us could get emotional over it." Even as battle-hardened veterans were assuming that civilians would be

shocked by such acts, however, the press in the United Sates contained evidence to the contrary. In April 1943, the *Baltimore Sun* ran a story about a local mother who had petitioned authorities to permit her son to mail her an ear he had cut off a Japanese soldier in the South Pacific. She wished to nail it to her front door for all to see. On the very same day, the *Detroit Free Press* deemed newsworthy the story of an underage youth who had enlisted and "bribed" his chaplain not to disclose his age by promising him the third pair of ears he collected.

Scalps, bones, and skulls were somewhat rarer trophies, but the latter two achieved special notoriety . . . when an American serviceman sent President Roosevelt a letter opener made from the bone of a dead Japanese (the president refused it), and *Life* published a full-page photograph of an attractive blond posing with a Japanese skull she had been sent by her fiancé in the Pacific. *Life* treated this as a human-interest story. . . . Another well-known *Life* photograph revealed the practice of using Japanese skulls as ornaments on U.S. military vehicles.[64]

Yet as shown above, Dower's account of the Pacific war does not at all rely on the kind of "monocausal explanation" that Goldhagen purports is the only plausible one. Note incidentally that, unlike the Americans, the Germans firmly forbade such publicity. "To every normal person," a German chief of staff lectured, "it is a matter of course that he does not take photographs of such disgusting excesses or report about them when he writes home. The distribution of photographs and the spreading of reports about such events will be regarded as a subversion of decency and discipline in the army and will be punished strictly." Indeed as Goldhagen suggests, those vio-

---

64. Dower, *War Without Mercy*, 65.

lating the Nazi taboo could suffer harsh penalties (*HWE:* 268, 585 n73).[65]

Returning to the main argument, nearly all the ordinary Germans assembled in the police battalions, according to Goldhagen, brutalized Jews with "gusto," "relish," "zeal," etc. Compare first the extreme case of "those soulless automata" (Höhne) staffing the concentration camps. "Among the guards there were some sadists, sadists in the pure clinical sense," Auschwitz survivor Dr. Victor Frankl recalled. Yet the "majority of the guards," although morally "dulled" by the relentless brutality of camp life, "refused to take active part in sadistic measures." The "sadists, brutal criminals . . . who enjoyed torturing human beings, and did it with passionate conviction," Auschwitz survivor Dr. Ella Lingens-Reiner similarly suggested in her memoir, were only a minority among several SS types in the camp. "Compared with our general living conditions," gratuitous cruelty "played an insignificant role. The deaths and cases of grave, permanent physical injury caused by those acts of brutality were, comparatively speaking, not so very numerous." "There were few sadists," Lingens-Reiner later testified at the Auschwitz trial. "Not more than five or ten percent." "Nothing would be more mistaken than to see the SS as a sadistic horde driven to abuse and torture thousands of human beings by instinct, passion, or some thirst for pleasure," concurred Auschwitz survivor Benedikt Kautsky. "Those who acted in this way were a small minority." Thus ordinary Germans were, if Goldhagen's thesis is correct, much more pathologically cruel than the concentration camp per-

---

65. Hilberg, *The Destruction of the European Jews,* vol. i, 325; Klee et al., *"The Good Old Days,"* 195ff. For the German photographs, cf. also Bartov, *Hitler's Army,* 104–5.

sonnel. Seen from Goldhagen's theoretical side, that would also make ordinary Germans much more in thrall to Nazi-like anti-Semitism than the camp guards.[66]

Amid the manifold repetitions of his sweeping generalization, Goldhagen suddenly reveals that its empirical basis is but fragmentary, indeed paper-thin.

> Few survivors have emerged, and so it is often up to the Germans to report their own brutality—however much there was—and thereby to incriminate themselves, which they are naturally reluctant to do. Moreover, the Federal Republic of Germany's investigating authorities were generally not interested in learning about instances of cruelty, since by the time of these investigations, all crimes, except murder, had passed the time limit for prosecution that is specified in the statute of limitations. No matter how much a German in a police battalion had beaten, tortured, or maimed a Jew, if he did not kill the victim, he could not be prosecuted for his actions. (*HWE:* 255; cf. 261)

---

66. Höhne, *The Order of the Death's Head,* 363; Frankl, *Man's Search for Meaning,* 92; Ella Lingens-Reiner, *Prisoners of Fear* (London, 1948), 129, 41 (cf. chap. 8, "The German S.S.," passim); Bernd Naumann, *Auschwitz* (New York, 1966), 91; Tzvetan Todorov, *Facing the Extreme* (New York, 1996), 122. Cf. also Sofsky, *The Order of Terror,* chap. 20. Ironically, Goldhagen chastises other historians for ignoring survivor testimony (cf. Goldhagen's review of Browning in *The New Republic,* 13–20 July 1992), yet on this—the crucial—point of his thesis, Goldhagen himself ignores what the classic survivor accounts report. For a clinical study that reaches the same conclusions as the survivors, cf. Zillmer et al., *The Quest for the Nazi Personality,* esp. 117, 119, 180–1. Regarding earlier versions of the Goldhagen thesis, Lingens-Reiner cautioned:

> When one report after the other focused the glare of its searchlight on the final horrors and the most outrageous atrocities, I began to feel . . . that something was missing, something therefore was wrong. Not that the most terrifying descriptions of inhuman cruelties and inhuman misery were not true! Yet, when the spotlight picked them out, it seemed to me that the background which made them possible, the day-to-day happenings and "normal" aspects of concentration camp life, became almost invisible and unintelligible. And if only the sensational horrors were registered, there was a danger that the far deeper, but less blatant, horror of the whole system would not be fully understood. (ix)

And again in an endnote:

> [T]he interrogations focus on establishing what crimes
> were committed and who committed them. The only
> crime with which all but the earliest investigations (and
> they were few and unrevealing) were concerned was mur-
> der, because the statute of limitations had expired for all
> other crimes. So the investigators were generally inter-
> ested in acts of cruelty only insofar as they were perpe-
> trated by the tiny percentage of perpetrators whom they
> indicted or believed they might indict, because such acts
> of cruelty would help to establish a perpetrator's motive;
> investigators, therefore, did not ask about or delve into
> the cruelties that the vast majority of perpetrators com-
> mitted. (*HWE:* 600 n5)

The actual documentation, according to Goldhagen, at best
"suggests" that gratuitous cruelty figured as a "part" of the
police battalions' repertoire (*HWE:* 255). The wonder would
be were it otherwise. Who ever doubted that there were sadis-
tically cruel Germans? To sustain his thesis, however, Goldhagen must prove considerably more. What marks off its
novelty, after all, is the audacious indictment of nearly all
battalion members—hence ordinary Germans—as sadistic
anti-Semites.

The evidentiary basis of Goldhagen's thesis is not only
exiguous. It is also highly selective. He categorically discounts
all "self-exculpating claims of the battalion men to opposition, reluctance, and refusal." Explaining his methodology,
Goldhagen recalls that criminals do not typically confess to
more than can be proven against them. What can be denied
is denied. Hence Goldhagen infers that the police battalions,
although acknowledging the genocide, concealed their sadism:
"Even when they could not completely hide that they had

given their bodies to the slaughter, they in all likelihood denied that they had given to it their souls, their inner will and moral assent" (*HWE:* 467–8, 534 n1). Leaving to one side the purely speculative nature of this claim, the fact is that the police battalions *did* openly confess to more—much more— than could have been proven against them.[67] Consider just a tiny sample of the incriminating admissions that Goldhagen reports:

> One killer even tells of a time he was sent alone with a Jew to the woods. He was under absolutely no supervision, so it was a perfect opportunity to let a victim flee, had he opposed the existing war of racist purgation. But he shot him. (*HWE:* 193)

> ". . . These Jews (men, women, and children) were crammed in the most inhumane manner in the available cars. . . . We had to leave the train at the final destination. . . . In the area we noticed a distinct smell of corpses. We could imagine what these people had to look forward to, and above all, that it was an extermination camp. We had previously been told that these people were being resettled." (*HWE:* 198)

> "I would like to mention now that only women and children were there. They were largely women and children around twelve years old. . . . I had to shoot an old woman, who was over sixty years old. I can still remember, that the old woman said to me, will you make it short or about the same." (*HWE:* 219)

> "I would like also to mention that before the beginning of the execution, Sergeant Steinmetz said to the members of the platoon that those who did not feel up to the upcom-

---

67. Note that, according to Browning, *Ordinary Men,* "there was a pronounced reluctance of the witnesses to criticize their former comrades" and that "such denunciations by the policemen, even of unpopular superiors, much less of their comrades, were extremely rare" (108, 151–2).

ing task could come forward. No one, to be sure, exempted himself." (*HWE: 220*)

"Thereupon the NCOs went to the edge of the forest, got themselves clubs, and then with these clubs rained mighty blows on the Jews . . . it is my opinion that all of the NCOs of our company complied with the . . . order and rained blows on the Jews." (*HWE: 228*)

"It is, moreover, true that there were always enough volunteers for the executions. I too volunteered once or twice for executions." (*HWE: 252*)

"I must admit that we felt a certain joy when we would seize a Jew whom one could kill. I cannot remember an instance when a policeman had to be ordered to an execution. The shootings were, to my knowledge, always carried out on a voluntary basis; one could have gained the impression that various policemen got a big kick out of it." (*HWE: 452*)

"I myself participated in ten killings during which I had to kill men and women." (*HWE: 540 n58*)

Indeed, Goldhagen's evidence of gratuitous brutality is culled almost entirely from the gratuitously self-incriminating testimony of the police battalions. Plainly this wasn't, by his own reasoning, typical criminal testimony. The police battalion members didn't seek at every opportunity to minimize their responsibility. Yet Goldhagen indiscriminately excludes all "self-exculpating" testimony on the assumption that they did.

It bears emphasis that the issue is not whether the testimony of the police battalions was riddled with lies, distortions, omissions, etc. Of course it must have been. The point rather is Goldhagen's *blanket* dismissal of all testimony impeaching his thesis. Thus he reports a police battalion member's gratuitous admission about killing Jewish patients in a hospital, while maintaining that the member's explanation that a superior officer threatened him "must be discounted" on principle (*HWE:* 200–1, 533 n74). Indeed Goldhagen highlights the absence of testimony that the police battalions dissented from this or that criminal act (*HWE:* 201). Yet all claims of dissent are anyhow automatically disregarded by him.

Acknowledging that the police battalions did initially recoil from their murderous assignment, Goldhagen nonetheless denies that this demurral at all registered moral qualms. Emphatically and repeatedly, he instead diagnoses the "unhappy, disturbed, perhaps even incensed" state of the police battalions as merely a "visceral reaction" to the "physically gruesome," "aesthetically unpleasant" task at hand: "The men were sickened by the exploded skulls, the flying blood and bone, the sight of so many freshly killed corpses of their own making." Contradicting himself, Goldhagen also states in the very same breath that the police battalions were "given pause, even shaken by having plunged into mass slaughter and committing deeds that would change and forever define them socially and morally" (*HWE:* 192, 220–2, 250, 252, 378, 400–1, 538 n39, 543 n98).

"Had this reaction been the consequence of principled opposition and not mere disgust," Goldhagen critically argues,

> the psychological strain would, with subsequent killings, have likely increased and not subsided completely. . . . But like medical students who might initially be shaken by their exposure to blood and guts yet who view their work as ethically laudable, these men easily adjusted to the unpleasant aspect of their calling. (*HWE:* 261)

Thus the police battalions' effortless psychological accommodation to the genocide demonstrates their Nazi-like anti-Semitism. Yet consider in this context Goldhagen's treatment of the Nazi "ideological exponents" recruited from the SS, SD, Gestapo, etc., to form the Einsatzgruppen.[68] As the genocide unfolded, the Einsatzgruppen *did* suffer, according to Goldhagen, escalating psychological distress. Goldhagen recalls the Nuremberg testimony of Einsatzgruppe commander Otto Ohlendorf: "I had sufficient occasion to see how many men of my Gruppe did not agree to this [genocidal] order in their inner opinion. Thus, I forbade the participation in these executions on the part of some of these men and I sent some back to Germany." On account of the severe emotional strain, Goldhagen further reports, "transfers occurred frequently" in the Einsatzgruppen and Himmler even issued explicit orders allowing for Einsatzgruppen members to excuse themselves. To explain why "the SS and security units were so lenient," Goldhagen also cites Himmler's assessment that the Judeocide "could only be carried out by . . . the staunchest individuals . . . [by] fanatical, deeply committed National Socialists." Goldhagen further highlights SS leader Reinhard Heydrich's orders that the Einsatzgruppen recruit local collaborators for the killings in order to "preserve the psychological equilibrium of our people" (*HWE:* 149, 380–1, 578–9 n13). Indeed precisely on this account, Goldhagen emphasizes, the Nazi leadership eventually switched to gas chambers:

Himmler, ever solicitous of the welfare of those who were turning his and Hitler's apocalyptic visions into deed,

---

68. For the Einsatzgruppen, cf. esp. *Trials of War Criminals Before the Nuernberg Military Tribunals,* vol. iv, "The Einsatzgruppen Case" (quoted phrase at 490).

began to search about for a means of killing that would be
less burdensome to the executioners. . . . The move to
gassing . . . —contrary to widely accepted belief—was
prompted not by considerations of efficiency, but by the
search for a method that would ease the psychological
burden of killing for the Germans. (*HWE:* 156–7; cf.
521 n81)

The severe disorientation of Einsatzgruppen members—
culminating in the breakdown of some and the barbarization
of others—and its repercussions for Nazi policy—the use,
e.g., of local collaborators, gas chambers, and military-style
executions to assuage the sense of individual guilt—are in fact
amply attested to in the documentary record. "Even Himmler's most aggressive Eastern minion," Höhne recalls,

> became a victim of the nightmare—von dem Bach-
> Zelewski was taken to the SS hospital . . . suffering from
> a nervous breakdown and congestion of the liver.
> Haunted by his guilt, he would pass his nights scream-
> ing, a prey to hallucinations. . . . The Head SS doctor
> reported to Himmler: "He is suffering particularly from
> hallucinations connected with the shootings of Jews in
> the East." (363)[69]

Goldhagen also suggests that the specific genocidal task
allotted the Einsatzgruppen was less stringent than that of the
police battalions: "The men in some of the police battalions

---

69. Cf. Breitman, *The Architect of Genocide,* 196–7, 204; Hilberg, *Perpetrators,
Victims, Bystanders,* 21, 55, 95; Hilberg, *The Destruction of the European Jews,* vol. i,
327–8, 332–3, vol. iii, 1008–10; Höhne, *The Order of the Death's Head,* 357, 363
(quote), 366–7; Klee et al., *"The Good Old Days,"* 5, 60, 68, 81–3, 129; *Trials of
War Criminals Before the Nuernberg Military Tribunals,* vol. iv, "The Einsatzgruppen Case," 183, 206, 245, 311.

had a more demanding, more psychologically difficult road to travel. Unlike the Einsatzkommandos, they were not eased into the genocidal killing, and integral to their operations was the emptying of ghettos of all life, with all the brutalities that it entailed" (*HWE: 277*).

Distilling the essence of Goldhagen's argument, we reach yet another truly novel conclusion:

> Ordinary Germans in the police battalions "easily adjusted" to the genocide;
> The specialized units in the Einsatzgruppen, although less morally taxed, experienced acute psychological strain;
> Ordinary Germans were much more Nazified than the Nazi ideological warriors in the Einsatzgruppen. QED

With the Red Army rapidly advancing on the Eastern front in the war's last stages, Himmler ordered the evacuation of the concentration camps. Goldhagen analyzes one of these "death marches" leaving off from the Helmbrechts camp. Even at the war's end and effectively left to their own devices, Goldhagen argues, ordinary Germans brutalized Jews.

The general significance of Goldhagen's case study is not at all clear. He first claims that there were "certain patterns and recurrent features of death marches." But then he immediately qualifies that the death marches were a "chaotic phenomenon, with sometimes significant variations in their character"; that "the disparities among the death marches were such that it would be hard to construct a persuasive model of them"; and that the death march was an "incoherent phenomenon" emerging out of the "chaos of the last months of the war" (*HWE: 364, 369*).

The guards leading the death marches were drawn from concentration camp personnel. One "typical" male guard, Goldhagen reports, was a Romanian of German ancestry who was ten years old when Hitler came to power. It is not immediately obvious what his sensibility might reveal about anti-Semitism in Germany before the Nazi era (*HWE:* 336–7). Goldhagen also reports that all the female guards belonged to the SS, at least half volunteers. Because they didn't enter the elite Nazi order until late 1944, he maintains, these female SS guards were nonetheless typical Germans. Yet so late in the war when defeat was in sight, arguably only fanatics would voluntarily embrace the Nazi cause.[70] To clinch his argument, Goldhagen recalls that "the head woman guard referred to them in her testimony as 'SS' guards with ironical quotation marks around 'SS.'" Wasn't Goldhagen's "methodological position," however, to "discount *all* self-exculpating testimony" (*HWE:* 337–8, 467, emphasis in original)?

Trying to cut a last-minute deal with the Americans, Himmler issued explicit orders not to kill the Jews. Yet "the Germans," Goldhagen observes, indulged in "multifarious cruel and lethal actions" against them. Indeed, "the purpose of the march in the minds of the guards, no matter what the higher authorities conceived it to have been, was to degrade, injure, immiserate, and kill Jews." Thus, the comparatively youthful female guards "were without exception brutal to the Jews." On the other hand, a survivor credited by Goldhagen recalls that "the older men of the guard unit were for the most part good-natured and did not beat or otherwise torment us. The younger SS men were far more brutal." But then "the

70. Bankier, *The Germans and the Final Solution,* 150.

Germans" were not a homogeneous lot. Indeed recall Goldhagen's claim that avowed Nazis were not more anti-Semitic than ordinary Germans and that the Hitler regime did not exacerbate anti-Semitism. But in a striking refutation of his thesis, the overall evidence cited by Goldhagen suggests that younger SS guards were much crueler than unaffiliated, older guards "bred not only on Nazi German culture" (*HWE:* 276, 337, 339, 346, 356–7, 360–1).

Goldhagen also adduces the guards' zigzag line of retreat as *prima facie* evidence of their sadistic anti-Semitism. The manifest intent was to further torture the Jews: "the aimlessness of the routes that they followed . . . suggest[s] that the marches, with their daily, hourly yield of debilitation and death, were their own reason for being," "viewing the maps . . . should be sufficient to convince anyone that the meanderings could have had no end other than to keep the prisoners marching. And the effects were calculable—and calculated," etc. (*HWE:* 365–6). Yet ten pages earlier Goldhagen reported that the guards

> had no prescribed route, so they had to feel their way towards some undetermined destination. They did not even possess a map. . . . As one guard states: "Throughout the march, the guards were unaware of where we were supposed to march to." The guards had to improvise constantly with the changing conditions. (*HWE:* 356)

It would seem that sadistic anti-Semitism is not the only plausible explanation for the "aimlessness" and "meanderings" of the death marches.

Even if Goldhagen's malignant spin on the evidence is credited, however, his thesis is scarcely proven. Just yesterday a heady dream, the Third Reich was for many Germans now a ghastly nightmare. The world had come crashing in. Abject surrender was only a matter of time. The archcriminal, archenemy Judeo-Bolsheviks of incessant Nazi propaganda were fast closing in. Judgment Day was at hand. Yet Himmler had ordered that the remnant Jews—these ambulatory skeletons of an evil past, these terrifying tokens of the vengeance to come—be kept alive. Some guards deserted (*HWE:* 360). Hating them and fearing them, wishing they would just die, the hardened and cowardly core tormented the Jews. The death march is, for Goldhagen, irrefutable proof that "situation factors were not what caused the Germans to act as they did" (*HWE:* 363). Yet is wanton brutality, under *these* circumstances, really so surprising?

Goldhagen also indicts the cruelty of German bystanders. He points up, for instance, the "frequent unwillingness of local German citizens" along the death march route to "spare food for Jewish 'subhumans'" (*HWE:* 365, 348). Yet in the directly ensuing narrative, Goldhagen recounts that— despite the "chaos and general food shortage of the time"—on the "first day of the march . . . , German civilians responded to the supplications of the Jews for food and water, only to meet the interdiction of the guards"; on the "seventh day, a town's Mayor proposed to accommodate the Jewish women in the hall that had been prepared with bedding for a large group of women auxiliaries of the German army who had been expected"; on the "eighth day . . . , a few women from Sangerberg tried to pass to the prisoners some bread. A male guard threatened one of the women who wanted to distribute food that he would shoot her if she should try again to pass food to the prisoners"; on the "sixteenth day . . . , [the guards] allowed the Jews to have some soup that the people of Althütten had prepared, but forbade them from receiving any other food"; and on the "twenty-first day . . . , the guards still refused to allow townspeople . . . to feed the Jews." Indeed, civilians "freely offered" food to Jews "throughout the march" (*HWE:* 348–9; cf. 365). To judge by Goldhagen's account, the truly noteworthy fact would seem to be not the infrequent but the frequent willingness of ordinary Germans even after twelve years of Nazi rule to reach out to Jews.[71]

"German children," recalls a survivor of the Helmbrechts death march, "began to throw stones at us." Clinching his thesis, Goldhagen concludes: "The German children, knowing nothing of Jews but what they learned from their society, understood how they were to act" (*HWE:* 365). Thus, to dispel any lingering doubt that pre-Nazi homicidal German anti-Semitism explains the Final Solution, Goldhagen points to German children stoning Jews in 1945.

VI.

Imbued as his study is with the imperatives of Holocaust literature, Goldhagen unsurprisingly harps on the categorical

---

71. Goldhagen's treatment of German anti-Semitism at war's end is typically disingenuous. From the multitude of immediate postwar surveys with their wildly contradictory findings, he culls only the most damning statistic. Thus he reports that "a survey done by American occupation authorities at the end of 1946 revealed that fully 61 percent of Germans were willing to express views that classified them as racists or antisemites" (*HWE:* 593 n53). But turning to the cited study, we also learn that, according to a survey a year earlier, fully 61 percent agreed that "the actions against the Jews were in no way justified" (Frank Stern, *The Whitewashing of the Yellow Badge* [Oxford, 1992], 117–8). For a sensitive appraisal of the postwar surveys, cf. Gordon, *Hitler, Germans, and the "Jewish Question,"* 197–209. Juxtaposing one finding that nearly 80 percent of Germans totally opposed Hitler's anti-Semitism against another (albeit in response to a "badly phrased question") that nearly 40 percent approved the extermination, Gordon concludes that no definitive conclusion is possible from these surveys.

uniqueness of the Nazi genocide.[72] Thus "there is no comparable event in the twentieth century, indeed in modern European history . . . the theoretical difficulty is shown by its
utterly new nature," "the Holocaust was a radical break with
everything known in human history . . . completely at odds
with the intellectual foundations of modern western civilization . . . as well as the . . . ethical and behavioral norms that
had governed modern western societies," etc. The perpetration of the genocide by the Germans accordingly "marked
their departure from the community of 'civilized peoples' "
(*HWE:* 4, 5, 28, 386, 419). No doubt facets of the Nazi
holocaust—for example, the annihilation centers (Treblinka,
Sobibor, etc.)—were unique. The case Goldhagen mounts,
however, sheds less light on the historical singularities of the
Judeocide than it does on his own singularly ahistorical sense.
It bears emphasis that the matter at issue is *not* whether the
crimes of the Nazi era were monumental. Rather it is whether
these monumental crimes are without *any* historical precedent
or parallel.

What distinguished Hitler's rule above all, according to
Goldhagen, was the concentration camp. It was the "emblematic," "novel," "distinctively new," "revolutionary" institution
of Nazi Germany, one that "most prominently set Germany
apart from other European countries, that to a large extent
gave it its distinctive murderous character," etc. (*HWE:* 170,
456–60). Yet as Hitler more or less accurately charged, "the
idea of concentration camps was born in British brains" during the Boer War. Some 150,000 women and children were
corralled in what pro-Boer British MPs dubbed at the time

---

72. I will return to this topic in the conclusion.

"concentration camps." In a litany that would soon become numbingly familiar, a contemporary witness to the Boer repression reported: "the wholesale burning of farms . . . the deportations . . . a burnt-out population brought by hundreds of convoys . . . deprived of clothes . . . the semi-starvation in the camps . . . the fever-stricken children lying . . . upon the bare earth . . . the appalling mortality." Fully a quarter of the internees eventually succumbed to measles, typhoid, and other pestilence.[73]

Recalling *Aktion Reinhard,* Goldhagen observes that "in the value-inverted world of Germany during the Nazi period, naming a genocidal undertaking after someone—in this case, the assassinated Reinhard Heydrich—was to honor him" (*HWE:* 532 n55). In an insane society like Nazi Germany's, a campaign of mass murder was named after a mass murderer. In a sane society like ours, the first atomic bomb, which killed two hundred thousand Japanese, was christened "Little Boy," and a program of mass assassination that left twenty thousand Vietnamese dead was named after the phoenix, the legendary symbol of rebirth and regeneration. In the "bizarre world" of Nazi Germany, Goldhagen highlights, more "solicitude" was shown for dogs than Jews: "The dog's fate . . . was greatly preferable to that of Jews. In every respect, Germans would have agreed, it was better to be a dog." Goldhagen goes on to observe that "any but those beholden to the Nazi creed" would have found such a state of affairs "deeply ironic and disturbing," "psychologically gripping, even devastating," etc. The "sensibilities" of these Nazified Germans, however, did not

---

73. Adolf Hitler, *My New Order* (New York, 1941), 777; Thomas Pakenham, *The Boer War* (New York, 1979), 522–4, 531–40, 548–9 (quote at 534). The phrase "concentration camps" was borrowed from the notorious *reconcentrado* camps set up by the Spanish to deal with the Cuban guerrillas.

"remotely approximate our own." They were "too far gone"; their "cognitive framework" was such that this "telling juxtaposition could not register" (*HWE*: 268–70). Yet foreigners visiting the United States are almost immediately struck that more solicitude is shown for pets than the homeless. Indeed the "cognitive framework" of many an American is such that the "telling juxtaposition" of supermarket aisles lined with pet food while twelve million children in the United States lack sufficient nutriments to sustain growth and development does not "register."[74]

The "perversity of the Nazified German mind was such," according to Goldhagen, that the deaths of German children during the Allied terror-bombing "did not . . . arouse sympathy" for Jewish children: "Instead, thinking of their children spurred the Germans to kill Jewish children" (*HWE*: 213). Recall that the attack on Pearl Harbor aroused no pangs of sympathy for the Japanese. "Japan's surprise attack," John Dower reports, "provoked a rage bordering on genocidal among Americans." The firebombing of Tokyo in 1945, which left some one hundred thousand civilians dead— "scorched and boiled and baked to death," in the words of the mastermind of the new strategy, Major-General Curtis LeMay—not only evoked "no sustained protest" but was "widely accepted as just retribution." The president's son and confidant, Elliott Roosevelt, supported bombing Japan "until we have destroyed about half the civilian population," while a key presidential advisor favored the "extermination of the Japanese in toto." Nearly one quarter of the respondents in a December 1945 *Fortune* magazine poll wished that the United

---

74. Noam Chomsky, *World Orders Old and New* (New York, 1994), 142.

States had the opportunity to use "many more" atomic bombs before Japan surrendered.[75]

An egregious feature of Nazism, Goldhagen emphasizes, was its racist underpinnings. In fact so aberrant were the racist ravings of Nazi Germany, according to Goldhagen, that "we" can barely grasp them:

> Germany during the Nazi period . . . operat[ed] according to a different ontology and cosmology, inhabited by people whose general understanding of important realms of social existence was not "ordinary" by our standards. The notion, for example, that an individual's defining characteristics were derived from his race and that the world was divided into distinct races . . . was an extremely widespread belief. That the world ought to be organized or reorganized according to this conception of an immutable hierarchy of races was an accepted norm. The possibility of peaceful coexistence among the races was not a central part of the cognitive landscape of the society. Instead, races were believed to be inexorably competing and warring until one or another triumphed or was vanquished. (*HWE:* 460; cf. 458)

For argument's sake, let us leave to one side Goldhagen's bizarre claim that judging an individual by his race and dividing the world into distinct races is "not 'ordinary' by our standards," indeed, is alien to our "ontology and cosmology." Yet even the racist Social Darwinism was very far from peculiar to Nazi Germany. Consider the views—altogether unexceptional until quite recently—of Theodore Roosevelt. "It is for the good of the world," opined one of the most revered twentieth-

---

75. Dower, *War Without Mercy,* 36, 40–1, 53–55.

century U.S. presidents, "that the English-speaking race in all its branches should hold as much of the world's surface as possible." Elaborating on this theme in his classic *Winning of the West,* Roosevelt reflected:

> The settler and pioneer have at bottom justice on their side; this great continent could not have been kept as nothing but a game preserve for squalid savages. . . .
>
> It is indeed a warped, perverse, and silly morality which would forbid a course of conquest that has turned whole continents into the seats of mighty and flourishing civilized nations. All men of sane and wholesome thought must dismiss with impatient contempt the plea that these continents should be reserved for the use of scattered savage tribes, whose life was but a few degrees less meaningless, squalid, and ferocious than that of the wild beasts with whom they hold joint ownership. . . .
>
> The most ultimately righteous of all wars is a war with savages, though it is apt to be also the most terrible and inhuman. The rude, fierce settler who drives the savage from the land lays all civilized man under a debt to him. . . .
>
> The world would probably not have gone forward at all, had it not been for the displacement or submersion of savage and barbaric peoples as a consequence of the armed settlement in strange lands of the races who hold in their hands the fate of the years. . . .

Or, as Roosevelt succinctly put it in his private correspondence, "if we fail to act on the 'superior people' theory, . . . barbarism and savagery and squalid obstruction will prevail over most of the globe."[76]

---

76. Theodore Roosevelt, *Winning of the West* (New York, 1889), vol. i, 119, vol. iv, 54–6; Elting E. Morison (ed.), *The Letters of Theodore Roosevelt* (Cambridge, 1951), vol. ii, 1176–7, vol. viii, 946. To justify the U.S. colonial war

The intent on killing, Goldhagen concludes, was *the* defining feature of the Nazi genocide: "It was the will and the motivation to exterminate European Jewry . . . the will . . . —that is the crucial issue." And again: "This issue—the issue of will—is the crucial issue." Goldhagen goes on to maintain that "*in this sense* [emphasis in original] the German perpetrators were like the perpetrators of other mass slaughters." Thus as in "any other mass slaughter or genocide," Germans killed because they "believed that they were right to kill." In fact it is a "grave error," Goldhagen warns, to assume that people cannot

> slaughter whole populations—especially populations that are by any objective evaluation not threatening—out of conviction. The historical record, from the ancient times to the present, amply testifies to the ease with which people can extinguish the lives of others, and even take joy in their deaths. (*Reply,* 44–5; *HWE:* 14)

---

in which more than two hundred thousand Filipinos were killed, Roosevelt observed: "The warfare that has extended the boundaries of civilization at the expense of barbarism and savagery has been one of the most potent factors in the progress of humanity" (*Presidential Addresses and State Papers of Theodore Roosevelt* [New York, 1970], vol. 1, 62–3). Denouncing the Nazis' racist *Weltanschauung,* the Nuremberg Tribunal repeatedly cited these words from a Hitler speech:

> But long ago man has proceeded in the same way with his fellowman. The higher race—at first higher in the sense of possessing a greater gift for organization—subjects to itself a lower race and thus constitutes a relationship which now embraces races of unequal value. Thus there results the subjection of a number of people under the will often of only a few persons, a subjection based simply on the right of the stronger, a right as we see it in nature can be regarded as the sole conceivable right because founded on reason.

Note that although plainly racist, Hitler's argument was but an anemic version of Roosevelt's. "Despite the gloomy aspect of history, with its wars, massacres, and barbarities," the Tribunal's final judgment read, "a bright light shines through it all if one recalls the efforts made in the past in behalf of distressed humanity." Two individuals are specifically lauded, the first being "President Theodore Roosevelt" (*Trials of War Criminals Before the Nuernberg Military Tribunals,* vol. iv, "The Einsatzgruppen Case," 33, 279, 497).

Yet Goldhagen also maintains that the Nazi genocide was singular precisely *because* Germans killed from "conviction" and a sense of "right":

> One of the remarkable features of the genocide . . . is how readily and naturally Germans . . . *understood* why they were supposed to kill Jews. . . . Antisemitism in Germany was such that when Germans . . . learned that the Jews were to be killed, they evinced not surprise, not incredulity, but comprehension. Whatever their moral or utilitarian stances towards the killing were, the annihilation of the Jews *made sense to them. (HWE:* 403, emphasis in original)

Leaving to one side this gross contradiction, yet another one leaps off the page. If the Nazi genocide was, on the "crucial issue," like "any other mass slaughter," it could not have marked "a radical break with everything known in human history." Indeed to judge by this account, it was a commonplace.

The circle is complete. From the mystifying premise that it was utterly new, through a welter of nonsensical assertions, misrepresentations, contradictions, and nonsequiturs, to the trivializing conclusion that it was utterly old: thus Daniel Jonah Goldhagen makes "sense" of the Nazi genocide.

3

Reflections on the Goldhagen Phenomenon

Hitler's Willing Executioners adds nothing to our current understanding of the Nazi holocaust. Indeed, recycling the long-discredited thesis of a sadistic "German mind," it *subtracts* from our understanding. As we have seen, Goldhagen's book is not scholarship at all. Between the gross misrepresentations of secondary literature and the glaring internal contradictions, it does not deserve consideration as an academic inquiry. Yet the book did indisputably elicit an avalanche of praise. How does one account for this paradox and what is its significance? I want to address these questions in two areas: scholarship and politics. It bears emphasis that, however informed, the remarks that follow are speculation. They clearly belong in a separate category from the preceding analysis of the text itself.

The Nazi extermination of the Jews gave rise to two parallel, indeed often contradictory, bodies of literature. In accord with the distinction signaled throughout this essay, one may speak of, respectively, holocaust scholarship, which tends to be historical and multicausal, and Holocaust literature, which tends to be ahistorical and monocausal. The line drawn marks off major tendencies, not absolute differences.[77]

Historians working within the holocaust field have gradually reached consensus that most ordinary Germans did not share Hitler's obsession with the Jews. A broad range of solid scholarly research has concluded that popular German anti-Semitism was only one among multiple factors behind Hitler's triumph and the Final Solution. In Holocaust literature the Nazi genocide is cast as the climax of a millennial Gentile hatred of Jews.[78] Hence the inference that popular German

---

77. The field of "Holocaust studies" straddles the divide.

78. One upshot is the Holocaust "uniqueness" mantra. In the Holocaust literature paradigm, the persecution of non-Jews in the Nazi holocaust becomes merely accidental and the persecution of non-Jews in history merely episodic. Thus the double claim in Holocaust literature that Jews suffered uniquely in the Nazi holocaust and the Nazi holocaust was unique in the annals of human suffering. From every standpoint Jewish suffering was unique. "Not to realize that the Jewish situation was unique," according to Yehuda Bauer, is "an inexcusable abomination based on the mystification of the event" (*The Holocaust in Historical Perspective* [Seattle, 1978], 36–8). "Auschwitz is a no-man's-land of understanding," maintains Dan Diner, "a black box of explanation, a vacuum of extrahistorical significance which sucks in attempts at historiographic interpretation" ("Between Aporia and Apology," in *Reworking the Past,* 144). For Alice L. and A. Roy Eckardt, the Holocaust was "essentially different from not only ordinary uniqueness but even unique uniqueness." It was an event of "transcending uniqueness . . . the quality of difference raises itself to the level of absoluteness" ("The Holocaust and the Enigma of Uniqueness," in *Annals of the American Academy* [July 1980], 168). The newest addition to the literature on Holocaust "uniqueness" is Steven T. Katz's *The Holocaust in Historical Context.* Citing nearly five thousand titles in the first of a projected three-volume study, Katz surveys the full sweep of human history in order to prove that "the Holocaust is phenomenologically unique by virtue of the fact that never before has a state set out, as a matter of intentional principle and actualized policy, to annihilate physically every man, woman, and child belonging to a specific people." Clarifying his the-

anti-Semitism *was* the mainspring of Hitler's success and the Jewish catastrophe that ensued. Ideological and politically driven, Holocaust literature is largely devoid of scholarly interest.[79] Virtually every seminal work seeking to recast the debate—e.g., Raul Hilberg's *The Destruction of the European Jews,* Hannah Arendt's *Eichmann in Jerusalem,* and Arno Mayer's *Why Did the Heavens Not Darken?*—has landed on the Holocaust literature index of forbidden texts.[80] The generic con-

---

sis, Katz explains: "ϕ is uniquely C. ϕ may share $A, B, D, \ldots X$ with Δ but not C. And again ϕ may share $A, B, D, \ldots X$ with all Δ but not C. Everything essential turns, as it were, on ϕ being uniquely C. . . . π lacking C is not ϕ. . . . By definition, no exceptions to this rule are allowed. Δ sharing $A, B, D, \ldots X$ with ϕ may be like ϕ in these and other respects . . . but as regards our definition of uniqueness any or all Δ lacking C are not ϕ. . . . Of course, in its totality ϕ is more than C, but it is never ϕ without C." To avoid any confusion, Katz further elucidates that he uses the term *phenomenologically* "in a non-Husserlian, non-Shutzean, non-Schelerian, non-Heideggerian, non-Merleau-Pontyan sense" (28, 58, 60). The fixation on Holocaust "uniqueness" has plainly broken the threshold—to paraphrase the Eckardts—not only of ordinary delirium, not only of delirious delirium, but even of transcendent, absolute delirium. Indeed it is not at all certain that the point at issue is scholarly. Peter Baldwin suggests a political motive to which I will return directly: "The singularity of the Jewish suffering adds to the moral and emotional claims that Israel can make on her citizens and on other nations" ("The *Historikerstreit* in Context," 21). For discussion of the Holocaust "uniqueness" thesis, cf. esp. David Stannard, "Uniqueness as Denial," in Alan Rosenblum (ed.), *Is the Holocaust Unique?* (Boulder, 1996), 163–208. Jean-Michel Chaumont's seminal study, *La Concurrence des victimes* (Paris, 1997), only first came to my attention after completing this manuscript. It more fully develops (albeit from a different angle) several of the themes adumbrated here.

79. See Raul Hilberg's scathing assessments in *The Politics of Memory* of two major representatives of this field—Lucy Dawidowicz, the doyenne of Holocaust literature in the United States, and Israel Gutman, director of the Research Center of Yad Vashem in Israel. For Dawidowicz's historical imagination, consider her claims that the "preoccupation" of American historiography with slavery rather than Jews is due to a "white Anglo-Saxon" bias, or that "American historians approaching the history of the Soviet Union" typically "neglect inquiry into political ideas and ideology" (*The Holocaust and the Historians,* 28, 30).

80. To be sure, the sins varied. Hilberg was blackballed for allegedly minimizing Jewish resistance. Yet the ideological phantom of formidable Jewish resistance only obscures the noninstrumental character of the Nazi genocide. Indeed, the claim of "Jewish partisan activity" was the Einsatzgruppen's main pretext for the slaughter. (For illuminating commentary on the ideological recasting of the

straints of Holocaust literature even seem to have corrupted the testimonial corpus. In point of fact, publication of almost all the sober and morally searching survivor accounts—those by Primo Levi, Viktor Frankl, and Ella Lingens-Reiner, for example—predates the emergence of Holocaust literature, which has created an intellectual climate conducive to more sensationalist and parochial memoirs.

The disciplinary division between holocaust scholarship— primarily a branch of European history—and Holocaust literature—primarily a branch of Jewish studies—was, until the publication of *Hitler's Willing Executioners,* mutually respected. For reasons not difficult to discern, neither side ventured too far afield: holocaust scholars steered clear of the political hornet's nest of Holocaust literature; defending and elaborating a particular fixed vision of the past, Holocaust literature firmly faced away from the findings of holocaust scholarship.[81]

Nazi holocaust to incorporate Jewish resistance, cf. Tom Segev, *The Seventh Million* [New York, 1993], 109–10, 179–80, 183–4, and esp. chap. 24, "Holocaust and Heroism.") The banishment of Hannah Arendt from the Holocaust fold for pointing up the crucial role of Jewish cooperation in the Final Solution is well known. Recent revelations concerning Arendt's relationship with Martin Heidegger have fueled new speculation. Thus Richard Wolin suggests that this affair was behind Arendt's "calumnies about the Jews" (*The New Republic,* 9 October 1995). Yet Arendt's indictment of Jewish collaboration pales beside that of Warsaw Ghetto Uprising leader Yitzak Zuckerman: "We didn't figure that the Germans would put in the Jewish element, that Jews would lead Jews to death" (*A Surplus of Memory* [New York, 1993], 210; cf. 192, 208–9, 212). Arno Mayer's main blasphemy was emphasizing the salience of anti-Bolshevism alongside anti-Semitism in Nazi ideology. The hatchet man in his case was then–Harvard graduate student Daniel Goldhagen (*The New Republic,* 17 April 1989).

81. In recent years, Holocaust literature has mushroomed into a veritable industry. In this regard Goldhagen breaks ground with the invention of a new subgenre: Holoporn. Consider this Goldhagen fantasy:

> The Germans made love in barracks next to enormous privation and incessant cruelty. What did they talk about when their heads rested quietly on their pillows, when they were smoking their cigarettes in those relaxing moments after their physical needs had been met? Did one relate to another accounts of a particularly amusing beating that she or he had administered or observed, of the rush of power that engulfed her when the righteous adrenaline of Jew-beating caused her body to pulse with energy? (*HWE:* 339)

Firmly anchored in the Holocaust literature paradigm, Goldhagen's book marks the first foray of a Holocaust ideologue across the divide into the holocaust field. In effect, Goldhagen wants to graft an ahistorical and monocausal thesis onto a body of historical and multicausal scholarship. The venture comes at a time when Holocaust literature is trying to entrench itself as a reputable area of scholarly inquiry. Indeed, Goldhagen himself is a candidate for the proposed chair in "Holocaust and Cognate Studies" at Harvard University.[82] Although it obscures the meaning of the Nazi genocide, Goldhagen's foray does cast a harsh if unwitting light on Holocaust literature. Seeking to reconcile an ideologically loaded thesis with radically incompatible empirical findings, Goldhagen cannot help but mangle the scholarly record and get mired in a morass of internal contradictions. What *Hitler's Willing Executioners* points to is the intellectual barrenness of Holocaust literature: ignoring as they do the findings of holocaust scholarship, the claims of Holocaust ideologues prove unsustainable when put to an empirical test.[83]

---

82. Revealingly, Holocaust studies has been exempted from the current mainstream assault on what is disparagingly dubbed "victim studies"—e.g., women's and gay and lesbian studies. The explanation for this discrepancy plainly is not comparative scholarly worth. One may also note that the field of Jewish studies has enjoyed comparable immunity from current mainstream attacks on ethnic studies—e.g., African-American and Latino studies.

83. Indeed, Goldhagen is to Holocaust literature what Elie Wiesel is to Holocaust memory. As the most prominent spokesperson for the monocausal reading of the past, and Goldhagen's main supporter, Wiesel merits special scrutiny. In a new memoir, *All Rivers Run to the Sea* (New York, 1995), Wiesel documents his credibility as a witness. Recently liberated from Buchenwald and only eighteen years old, he reports, "I read *The Critique of Pure Reason*—don't laugh!—in Yiddish." Leaving aside Wiesel's acknowledgment that at the time "I was wholly ignorant of Yiddish grammar" (139, 163–4), *The Critique of Pure Reason* was never translated into Yiddish. Wiesel also recalls in intricate detail a "mysterious Talmudic scholar" who "mastered Hungarian in two weeks, just to surprise me" (121–30). These instances, though extraordinary, are in themselves relatively minor. But on a much more serious level, Wiesel elsewhere in the memoir rebukes a skeptical critic by saying that he who "refuses to believe me" is "lend-

Holocaust literature first flourished in the wake of the June 1967 Arab-Israeli war. This is the crucial political context for comprehending the Goldhagen phenomenon. It is a fact seldom noticed that, until the June war, Israel and Zionism occupied a marginal place in American Jewish intellectual life. In the wake of Israel's victory and its realignment with U.S. power, Jewish intellectuals suddenly discovered the Jewish state, now celebrated as a guardian of Western civilization, doing battle on the front lines with the Arab hordes and, against all odds, smashing them. Many also suddenly discovered the Nazi genocide.[84] Though only a tiny cottage industry originating at the time of the Eichmann trial, Holocaust literature boomed after the 1967 war. "By the late Sixties," reports Geoff Eley, "the term 'Holocaust' was appearing regularly in the titles of essays and books, freshly equipped with both a

---

ing credence to those who deny the Holocaust" (336). The moral sensibility of Wiesel is on a par with his memory. Denouncing the very mention, alongside the six million Jews, of the five million non-Jews (Gypsies, Soviet POWs, homosexuals, etc.) who also perished in the Nazi camps, Wiesel opines that the eleven million figure lacks "any kind of historical or ethical truth" (*Against Silence* [New York, 1984], vol. ii, 243; cf. vol. iii, 146). The June 1982 Israeli invasion of Lebanon costing the lives of some twenty thousand people was, according to Wiesel, a mere blip on the historical screen without moral consequence: "I believe one cannot judge an ancient people on the basis of episodes. We are a 4,000-year-old people, and what we do today reflects a history of 4,000 years. Episodes are episodes." Condemning Jews who opposed the indiscriminate bombing of Lebanon's capital city for "spreading confusion," Wiesel rather suggests: "Would it not have been better to have offered Israel unreserved support, regardless of the suffering endured by the population of Beirut?" (*Against Silence,* vol. ii, 213, 216).

84. In Alexander Bloom's *Prodigal Sons* (New York, 1986), a richly detailed portrait of the New York Jewish intellectual scene through the late 1960s, there is scarcely a mention of either Zionism or Israel. The memoirs of prominent American Jewish intellectuals across the political spectrum confirm that "none of us were Zionists" (Sidney Hook, *Out of Step* [New York, 1987], 5), that "the Six-Day War probably formed a turning point" (Irving Howe, *A Margin of Hope* [New York, 1982], 277), and that Israel after the June war was "now the religion of the American Jews" (Norman Podhoretz, *Breaking Ranks* [New York, 1979], 335).

capital letter and the definite article."[85] The version of the Nazi genocide gaining currency conceived it not as a complex and contingent event but rather as a uniquely Jewish event perpetrated in the name of eternal anti-Semitism. It is hard not to see significance in the confluence of these developments. Basking as they were in Israel's reflected glory, American Jews had also to contend with the danger of an increasing censure of its repressive policies. In this climate, the idea of an ineradicable anti-Semitism was bound to find fertile ground. Explaining criticism of Israel, Irving Howe, for example, gestured to that "sour apothegm: *In the warmest of hearts there's a cold spot for the Jews.*"[86]

Anti-Semitism, according to Zionist ideology, expresses the Gentile's natural and irreconcilable animus for Jews. The Nazi genocide marks in this reading the ineluctable culmination of Gentile anti-Semitic hatred.[87] Thus interpreted, the Nazi extermination both justifies the necessity of Israel and accounts for all hostility directed at it: the Jewish state is the

---

To cite one illustrative example, *Dissent* magazine devoted only two or three articles to Israel from its founding in 1954 through the 1967 war. Yet in subsequent years, *Dissent* editors Irving Howe and Michael Walzer were seen as intellectual mainstays of the Jewish state. One may further note that the only allusions in *Dissent* before the June war to the Nazi holocaust were two critical reviews of Hannah Arendt's *Eichmann in Jerusalem* and an article commemorating the Warsaw Ghetto Uprising.

85. Geoff Eley, "Holocaust History," in *London Review of Books,* 3–16 March 1982.

86. *New York* magazine, 24 December 1973 (emphasis in original).

87. Zionism posits—in Hannah Arendt's words—"a doctrine of eternal anti-semitism governing the relations of Jews and Gentiles everywhere and always," indeed, "the eternal and ubiquitous nature of anti-Semitism [has] been the most potent ideological factor in the Zionist movement" (Hannah Arendt, *The Jew as Pariah,* ed. Ron H. Feldman [New York, 1978], 141; Hannah Arendt, *Eichmann in Jerusalem* [New York, 1980], 10). The Nazi holocaust, as Omer Bartov points out, is for Zionism "taken therefore almost as a given, as a natural law, as being anything but surprising. If not ordered by God, it was at least an historical inevitability" (*Murder in Our Midst* [New York, 1996], 60).

only safeguard against the next outbreak of homicidal anti-Semitism and, conversely, homicidal anti-Semitism is behind every attack on, or even defensive maneuver against, the Jewish state. "The Holocaust" is in effect the Zionist account of the Nazi holocaust. And it acquired special status after the June 1967 war because it was politically expedient. Politically inexpedient was the scholarly consensus showing that most ordinary Germans did not elect or later support Hitler primarily because of his anti-Semitism, indeed, that they didn't evince support for Nazi violence or the Nazi genocide.

In this light, key elements of Goldhagen's study take on new resonance. "Without a doubt . . . the all-time leading form of prejudice and hatred within Christian countries," anti-Semitism, according to Goldhagen, "has been a more or less *permanent* feature of the western world." Effectively derogating all other forms of bigotry, Goldhagen thus endows anti-Semitism with a unique ontology, one that virtually defies historical analysis. We have already seen that, for Goldhagen, where anti-Semitism is not manifest it may yet be latent,[88] and that anti-Semitism and even philo-Semitism "tend strongly toward a genocidal 'solution.' "[89] Thus all Gen-

---

88. The "traditionally Zionist feeling," Hannah Arendt observed, is that "all Gentiles are anti-Semitic, and everybody and everything is against the Jews, that, in the words of Herzl, the world can be divided into *verschämte und unverschämte Antisemiten*"—i.e., overt and covert anti-Semites. Although in classical Zionist formulations, anti-Semitism would cease once Jews in-gathered in their own state, "general Gentile hostility . . . is now assumed by Zionists to be an unalterable eternal fact of Jewish history that repeats itself under any circumstances." Arendt significantly concludes: "Obviously this attitude is plain racist chauvinism and it is equally obvious that this division between Jews and all other peoples—who are to be classed as enemies—does not differ from other master race theories" (Hannah Arendt, "To Save the Jewish Homeland," in *Commentary*, May 1948, 401). Note, incidentally, what was permissible in *Commentary*'s pages before the June 1967 war. (I am indebted to John Murray Cuddihy, *The Ordeal of Civility* [New York, 1987], 78, for directing me to this reference.)

89. Goldhagen locates "eliminationist antisemitism"—i.e., the tendency toward extermination—in Germany. Yet in his formulation, it must be a general

tiles are potential if not actual homicidal anti-Semites. The subtitle of Goldhagen's book is "Ordinary Germans and the Holocaust," but the subtext is "Ordinary Gentiles and the Holocaust."

Going beyond classical Zionist, let alone standard scholarly, analyses, Goldhagen also purports that anti-Semitism "is always *abstract* in its conceptualization and its source." He conceives anti-Jewish animus as "divorced from actual Jews," "fundamentally *not* a response to any objective evaluation of Jewish action," "independent of the Jews' nature and actions," etc. Indeed, according to Goldhagen, anti-Semitism is strictly a Gentile mental pathology: its "host domain" is "the mind" (*HWE:* 34–5, 39, 42, emphases in original).

It should be clear that, in the context of the Nazi genocide, there can be no question of Jewish guilt or innocence. That is what makes Goldhagen's overarching framework—absolute Gentile guilt, complete Jewish innocence—convincing to many readers. Yet by proposing a transhistorical explanation for the Nazi holocaust, Goldhagen effectively detaches the most extreme manifestation of anti-Semitism from its historical context. Anti-Semitism becomes a chronic mental aberration "divorced from actual Jews" and it follows that at all times and for no reason, Gentiles harbor homicidal anti-Jewish animus, while Jews always enjoy a priori moral impunity. That ahistorical conception is of evident utility to those who maintain that all critiques of Zionism are simply disguised forms of anti-Semitism. The Jewish state is accordingly immunized from legitimate censure of its policies: all criticism is and must be motivated by fanatical anti-

---

tendency. At any rate, Goldhagen never specifies why it was peculiar to Germany. To adduce the Nazi holocaust as evidence is plainly a *post hoc, ergo propter hoc* argument. Indeed, as shown above, Goldhagen never grounds "eliminationist antisemitism" in German history.

Semitism.[90] Intent as Gentiles always are on murdering Jews, Jews have every right to protect themselves however they see fit; whatever expedient Jews might resort to, even aggression and torture, constitutes legitimate self-defense. Thus Goldhagen confers on Jews a double exoneration: total blamelessness and total license.[91]

One cannot but be struck by the parallels between the Goldhagen phenomenon and an earlier ideologically serviceable best-seller, Joan Peters's *From Time Immemorial* (New York, 1984), which maintained that Palestine was literally empty on the eve of Zionist colonization. In both cases: (1) a relative unknown claimed to scoop a stodgy, benighted aca-

---

90. Consider, for instance, Elie Wiesel's depiction of Jews as the eternally blameless victims of fanatical Gentile hatred. "How is one to live and hope in a world which, time and time again, tries to make us lower our heads? What do they want of us? How is one to live and pray in a world which forever sees in us a reminder of its own guilt? What is the use of continuing to believe in man if his face is relentlessly twisted in hate and madness?" "For two thousand years the Jewish people lived on the edge of extinction. We were always threatened; somewhere Jews were always being killed. For what? For no reason." "Mankind has betrayed us, but we have never betrayed mankind." "For centuries we proclaim our faith in humanity, and mankind tries to prove to us that we are wrong." (*Against Silence,* vol. i, 247, 255, 314, 349; cf. vol. i, 161, 209, 260–1, 283, 375, 378)

Therefore, according to Wiesel, all criticism of the Jewish state is motivated by this fanatical Gentile hatred. "Because of who we are and what our homeland Israel represents—the heart of our lives, the dream of our dreams—when our enemies try to destroy us, they will do so by trying to destroy Israel. And they will try to destroy Israel by destroying us. Can we guarantee that Israel will be in peace after its many sacrifices? No, we cannot. Can we guarantee that even if we give up our territories we shall be secure? No, we cannot. Can we guarantee that if we are morally right there will be no more Nazis in the world? No, we cannot. What we are, what we have stood for over the centuries has never been a deterrent to our enemies. In fact, the more we have loved life and the more we have loved justice and human dignity, the more we have been persecuted" (*Against Silence,* vol. i, 384; cf. vol. i, 209, 237, 247, 305). Apart from Gentile hatred, Wiesel does allow that criticism of Israel may be due to the fact that "we are coming closer to the year 2000, and something in the flow of history frightens man as he nears the millennium" (*Against Silence,* vol. i, 384).

91. A full discussion of the origins of the Holocaust industry would also have to include domestic influences. Aligned with black people against the Jim Crow

demic establishment. Peters was an occasional journalist, Goldhagen a recent Harvard Ph.D.; (2) the scholarly breakthrough was actually a caricatured version of a stale, Zionist thesis long repudiated in the academic literature; (3) purporting as it did to be an academic study, the book had to cite the documentary record and extant scholarship, both of which pointed to the opposite conclusion. Thus the evidence adduced in support of the novel thesis either was grossly misrepresented or else actually gainsaid the thesis; (4) prominent scholars with no specialized knowledge of the field launched the ideological enterprise. Peters's book jacket featured ful-

---

system in the South, many Jews broke with the Civil Rights alliance in the late 1960s when the struggle for equality no longer turned on caste discrimination but rather economic privilege. Articulating the class outlook of an ethnic group that had largely "made it" in the United States, Jewish neoconservatives figured prominently in the assault on the poor. Playing the Holocaust card to deflect criticism, Jewish neocons wrapped themselves in the cloak of virginal innocence and invoked black anti-Semitism at every turn. On the other hand, former Jewish leftists joining the political mainstream exploited the Holocaust as they tarred the New Left with charges of anti-Semitism.

Consider in this connection the aperçus of Elie Wiesel. Although "the blacks" appropriated "Holocaust terms of reference" like "ghetto," "genocide," and "mass murder," deplored Wiesel, "they do not thank us but attack us."

We find ourselves in a very dangerous situation. We are again the scapegoat on all sides. There are streets where it is dangerous for a man to walk, especially if he is a Jew. I read in the paper yesterday that the blacks beat up a rabbi. And you know the things that the blacks are saying on the television, on the radio, in the papers. It is terrible. I am really afraid. On the other hand, what is to be done? We helped the blacks; we always helped them. Should we stop helping them? This is a very tough problem. . . . I feel sorry for the blacks. There is one thing they should learn from us and that is gratitude. No people in the world knows gratitude as we do; we are forever grateful. (*Against Silence,* vol. iii, 202, 222)

Jews in the New Left, Wiesel further lamented, "attack Israel viciously. They call the Israelis aggressors in order to ingratiate themselves among the Leftists." And again: "If you are against Israel today you are *ipso facto* anti-Jewish. And if you are a Jew and against Israel, you are a renegade. The Jewish kids in the New Left . . . must be proclaimed openly and publicly renegades of the Jewish people. Let them do what they want. But they should not be part of the Jewish people. They are not" (*Against Silence,* vol. i, 262, vol. iii, 197–8).

In Wiesel's view, incidentally, all the upheavals of the 1960s—"the blacks," "the student revolt," even "LSD"—were "linked with the Holocaust" (*Against Silence,* vol. i, 251, 280, vol. iii, 202).

some blurbs by Lucy Dawidowicz ("the historical truth") and Barbara Tuchman ("a historical event"); Goldhagen's book jacket has blurbs by Simon Schama ("phenomenal scholarship and absolute integrity") and Stanley Hoffmann ("truly revolutionary . . . impeccable scholarship . . . profound understanding"); (5) once the ideological juggernaut achieved sufficient momentum, what little mainstream media criticism there was subsided.[92]

Touted as the ultimate testament to the Nazi holocaust, *Hitler's Willing Executioners* in fact fundamentally diminishes its moral significance. For what is the essence of Goldhagen's thesis if not that only deranged perverts could perpetrate a crime so heinous as the Final Solution? Lurid as Goldhagen's account is, the lesson it finally teaches is thus remarkably complacent: normal people—and most people, after all, *are* normal—wouldn't do such things. Yet the overwhelming majority of SS guards, Auschwitz survivor Dr. Ella Lingens-Reiner testified after the war, were "perfectly normal men who knew the difference between right and wrong." "We must remember," Auschwitz survivor Primo Levi wrote, that "the diligent executors of inhuman orders were not born torturers, were not (with a few exceptions) monsters: they were ordinary men." Not deranged perverts but "perfectly normal men," "ordinary men": *that* is the really sensational truth about the perpetrators of the Final Solution.[93]

---

92. For the Joan Peters hoax, cf. Edward Said and Christopher Hitchens (eds.), *Blaming the Victims* (New York, 1988), chap. 1, and Finkelstein, *Image and Reality of the Israel-Palestine Conflict,* chap. 2. Although both books were deluged with media praise, *From Time Immemorial* fared rather better than *Hitler's Willing Executioners* among academic specialists. One reason is as obvious as it is telling: while the holocaust field sustains impressive scholarly standards, Middle East studies is partly driven by the same ideological agenda as Holocaust literature.

93. Naumann, *Auschwitz,* 91; Primo Levi, *The Reawakening* (New York, 1965), 214. Cf. Primo Levi, *The Drowned and the Saved,* 121–2, 202–3. Thus also Han-

"From our findings," observed the American psychiatrist responsible for the Nuremberg defendants,

> we must conclude not only that such personalities are not unique or insane, but also that they could be duplicated in any country of the world today. We must also realize that such personalities exist in this country and that there are undoubtedly certain individuals who would willingly climb over the corpses of one half of the people of the United States, if by so doing, they could thereby be given control of the other half.

In fact the men sitting in the dock at Nuremberg constituted Germany's, as it were, "best and brightest." Of the twenty-one Nazi leaders indicted at the Trial of German Major War Criminals, six scored "superior" and twelve "very superior" on the IQ test. Truly these were the "whiz kids" of Germany. Or consider the Nazi elite murderers sitting in the dock at the Einsatzgruppen trial. "Each man at the bar," recalled the Nuremberg Tribunal in its final judgment,

> has had the benefit of considerable schooling. Eight are lawyers, one a university professor, another a dental physician, still another an expert on art. One, as an opera singer, gave concerts throughout Germany before he began his tour of Russia with the Einsatzkommandos. This group of educated and well-bred men does not even lack a former minister, self-frocked though he was. Another of the defendants, bearing a name illustrious in the world of music, testified that a branch of his family

---

nah Arendt famously assessed Eichmann: "The trouble with Eichmann was precisely that so many were like him, and that the many were neither perverted nor sadistic, that they were, and still are, terribly and terrifyingly normal" (*Eichmann in Jerusalem*, 276).

reached back to the creator of the "Unfinished Symphony." . . .[94]

"The most refined shedders of blood," Dostoyevsky long ago recognized, "have been almost always the most highly civilized gentlemen," to whom the official criminal misfits "could not have held a candle." Indeed, fixating as it does on the pathologically criminal, *Hitler's Willing Executioners* fails to even grasp, let alone resolve, the central mystery of the Nazi holocaust: how, under particular historical circumstances, ordinary men and women, as well as the "civilized gentlemen" who lead nations, can commit history's greatest crimes.

------

94. Zillmer et al., *The Quest for the Nazi Personality*, 48, 79; *Trials of War Criminals Before the Nuernberg Military Tribunals*, vol. iv, "The Einsatzgruppen Case," 500.

Part Two

REVISING

THE HOLOCAUST *

Ruth Bettina Birn

(in collaboration with
Dr. Volker Riess)

* The views expressed in this essay are those of the author and not those of the Department of Justice, Canada.

I.

Questions about the motives of the perpetrators and, by implication, the causes of the Holocaust, have long been in the forefront of academic or nonacademic discussions of the Nazi period—from the time of contemporary observers to the present day.* A wide range of possible responses to these ques-

---

* This article originally appeared in *The Historical Journal* (40, 1, 1997), 195–215. Its republication in a book aimed at a broader readership necessitated linguistic and stylistic changes. I am grateful to Sara Bershtel of Metropolitan for these editorial suggestions. A paragraph quoting from *Hitler's Willing Executioners* has been omitted from page 126 since it is cited in the other contribution to this volume. In fall 1997, Daniel Goldhagen published a reply to my article entitled "The Fictions of Ruth Bettina Birn" (*German Politics and Society* [15, 3, 1997], hereafter *Goldhagen 1997*). I am indebted to Daniel Goldhagen for pointing out two errors that have now been corrected (in one case internal quotation marks

tions has been put forward, drawing on concepts from a variety of disciplines, such as history, psychology, sociology, or theology. Daniel Goldhagen's book on the motivation of the perpetrators of the Holocaust claims to be a "radical revision of what has until now been written" (9). This claim is made on the book jacket and by the author himself. His thesis can be summarized as follows: Germany was permeated by a particularly radical and vicious brand of anti-Semitism whose aim was the elimination of Jews. The author defines this as "eliminationist antisemitism." This viral strain of anti-Semitism, he states, "resided ultimately in the heart of German political culture, in German society itself" (428). Medieval anti-Semitism, based as it was on the teachings of the Christian religion, was so "integral to German culture" (55) that with the emergence of the modern era it did not disappear but rather took on new forms of expression, in particular, racial aspects. By the end of the nineteenth century "eliminationist antisemitism" dominated the German political scene. In the Weimar Republic, it grew more virulent even before Hitler came to power. The Nazi machine merely turned this ideology into a reality. The course of its actualization was not deterred by anything save bare necessity: "the road to Auschwitz was not twisted" (425). When the "genocidal program" was implemented along with the German attack on the Soviet Union, it was supported by the general German population, by the "ordinary Germans"—the key phrase of the book—who became "willing executioners." They had no need for special orders, coercion, or pressure because their "cognitive model" showed them that Jews were "ultimately fit only to suffer and to die" (316).

---

were dropped; in the second, external quotation marks were overlooked). He also raises several issues that I have taken the opportunity of clarifying in footnotes inserted at relevant junctures in this text. These notes bear asterisks.

Daniel Goldhagen's book has become an international event. He has been interviewed and quoted, appeared on TV, and traveled widely to discuss his work. Reviews, both enthusiastic and critical, have poured from the presses in many countries. It is hard to think of a large academic book that has had such a reception and even harder to explain why. The book itself is made up of three parts: an overview of German history and the significance of anti-Semitism therein, three case studies, and roughly one hundred pages of conclusions. The first, general section has been the subject of most of the attention of reviewers. This essay will, therefore, concentrate on the case studies, the sources that Goldhagen has used and the methodology on which the book rests. I only want say one thing with respect to the general issues that Goldhagen raises. His assertion that German anti-Semitism was unique can only be made by comparing it to other forms of anti-Semitism. If one claims that only Jews were treated in a special way, one has to analyze the treatment of other victims; if one claims that only Germans committed certain deeds, one has to compare them to the deeds of non-Germans. If one claims that *all* Germans acted in a certain way, as Goldhagen does, it is insufficient to base one's conclusions on three groups of perpetrators; rather one has to compare the behavior of different groups in German society. It is odd that a professor of political science makes no attempt to look at his evidence in a comparative framework.

The evidence itself has not been examined by reviewers, because most of them are not familiar with Goldhagen's sources. In fact, the author uses historical documents only to a minimal extent; apart from some Nuremberg documents and a few files from the German Federal Archives, he relies mainly on secondary literature. For his case studies, he uses material mainly from German postwar investigations of Nazi crimes, which are, for the most part, to be found in the Central

Agency for the Prosecution of Nazi Crimes[1] in Ludwigsburg, Germany.

The importance of investigation and trial records for research on the Nazi period has been recognized by scholars for more than twenty-five years. However, historians also appreciate that these records must be interpreted critically. Not only are witness statements recollections of things past, and therefore subject to retrospection, but in a criminal investigation, additional incentives for distorting the truth exist. Goldhagen's methodology for dealing with statements of perpetrators is to "discount all self-exculpating testimony that finds no corroboration from other sources." The bias created by this selection he considers "negligible" (467; cf. 601 n11).

This approach is too mechanical and inadequate for dealing with the complexities of the issue, in particular since Goldhagen's stated aim is to study the complex motivational aspects of murder. Statements about motives form an integral part of a perpetrator's testimony, and evaluating them is not as easy as sorting out corroborated from uncorroborated facts. A number of other variables have to be considered: (1) the context of the investigation (great differences exist between individual investigations, in part due to the investigative body responsible when the investigation took place, in part due to contrived testimonies), (2) the context of the statement (perpetrators often gave different statements in different settings and at different times, which can differ considerably in content), (3) the manner in which the statement was recorded (statements in the German legal system are not verbatim transcriptions, but a summary prepared by the interrogator; they are not the

---

1. Abbreviated as ZStL.

words of the person himself, and only in some cases are direct quotations inserted).

A comparative approach is imperative when evaluating interrogations. Only by reviewing as broad a base of statements as possible are discrepancies, distortions, and omissions likely to be revealed. Moreover, only the comparative method can place the statements into their proper historical, and individual, context and allow for informed conclusions. In this respect, Goldhagen's study falls short. His evidentiary base is extremely small; for each of his major topics, he has concentrated on only one investigation, or parts of several investigations. The number of statements on which he bases his conclusions is fewer than two hundred, which is a very narrow selection from the tens of thousands of statements in existence on those topics. In addition, he uses only snippets of indictments, verdicts, or case summaries by German prosecutors. He also uses portions of statements from a wide range of investigations that are unrelated to the topics he discusses in the book. In light of this paucity of sources, it is not surprising that Goldhagen's book has neither a bibliography nor a listing of archival sources.

II.

The empirical evidence which Goldhagen marshals in support of his hypothesis deals with three aspects of the Nazi era: (*a*) the Order Police, specifically the Police Battalions,[2] (*b*) Jewish labor, and (*c*) the death marches.

---

2. The Order Police refers to the ordinary uniformed police, which comprised both stationary units in police precincts and mobile police battalions.

Goldhagen rightly deplores the fact that a comprehensive history of the Order Police in the Nazi period has not as yet been written. The participation of the Order Police in the Holocaust has, however, been dealt with in the major general histories of the Holocaust, as for instance by Raul Hilberg in *The Destruction of the European Jews,* or by Browning in his recent study of Police Battalion 101.[3] Goldhagen, while contending that Police Battalions provide "an unusually clear window" (181) for the understanding of the genocide, does not think a "thorough comprehension of institutional development" (181) necessary for his analysis. Consequently, he has not dealt with any of the extensive materials on the Order Police (apart from four files from the R 19 collection in the Bundesarchiv Koblenz), though he could have avoided a number of basic mistakes through a closer acquaintance with the subject.

Goldhagen's argument asserts the following: police battalions were the "organizational home of a large number of Germans" (182), who were "randomly selected" (183); these battalions were "populated by neither martial spirits nor Nazi supermen" (185). In order to substantiate his assertions, he examines the members of one battalion, "Polizeibataillon 101," in greater detail.[4] Its members, when sent to eastern Poland in 1942, were mainly reservists. They were older men, neither overproportionally party members nor SS members, and, as Goldhagen argues, their collective social backgrounds are such that they can be seen as a representative sample of German society as a whole. They are, he says, "representative

---

3. Christopher R. Browning, *Ordinary Men: Reserve Police Battalion 101 and the Final Solution in Poland* (New York, 1992).

4. According to Goldhagen, 550 men are known to have served in Police Battalion 101. He has birthdates for 519 of them. He has additional information, including occupation, for only 291 (206, 535).

of German society—that is, ordinary Germans—in their degree of Nazification" (207). Despite the controversy in the social sciences over the presumed correlation between a person's social background and behavior in a given situation, Goldhagen turns presumption into premise by abandoning all pretense of examining empirical data. He boldly asserts that an examination of this one battalion allows for insight into the "likely conduct of other ordinary Germans" (208). This leap from a limited quantity to a collective quality, by which real events are grossly relativized, is rather breathtaking. Significantly, the book's analysis does not include other police battalions that were also active in the Holocaust and were not comprised of reservists but of career police officers or volunteers.[5]

Goldhagen's argument develops in the following way: the statements of former members of Police Battalion 101 disclose an incident in which the commander, Major Trapp, explicitly told his men that they did not have to shoot if they did not want to. This was on the occasion of the unit's first mass shooting of Jews. Obviously, the commander here is unwilling to comply with his orders. A few men availed themselves of the offer not to shoot; the majority did not. This raises the obvious question of the complying men's motives. The motivating force for compliance was, according to Goldhagen, the "great hatred for the Jews" (425). Goldhagen suggests that the men took part because they wanted to kill, and, in one of his many extrapolations to all police battalions, he states that one can "generalize with confidence [that] by choosing not to

---

5. For instance: Police Reserve Battalion 45, ZStL SA 429 Indictment StA Regensburg I 4 Js 1495/65; Police Battalion 306, ZStL SA 447 Verdict LG Frankfurt 4 Ks 1/71; Battalion 316, ZStL, SA 387, Verdict LG Bochum 15 Ks 1/66.

excuse themselves . . . the Germans in police battalions themselves indicated that they wanted to be genocidal executioners" (279).

During the investigation into their activities, members of
Police Battalion 101 gave explanations for their behavior.
These form the core of Christopher Browning's study, and they
point toward a different interpretation of motivation from
that supplied by Goldhagen, particularly with respect to the
first mass execution. By and large, the men were not eager to
conduct the mass-killing operation, a fact which is corroborated by those who remained behind and did not shoot.
But they did participate in the executions nevertheless. Over
time, as the mass killings continued, certain character types
emerged: the very few who continued to stand apart; those
who enjoyed the killing, volunteered, and thus gave free reign
to their sadistic impulses; and those who simply continued
to commit mass murder and grew increasingly barbaric.
Browning discusses a wide range of explanations for this
behavior, based on sociopsychological concepts, and argues
that the most likely explanation is a mixture of peer pressure,
careerism, and obedience.

In order to support his hypothesis, Goldhagen is forced to
reject not only Browning's interpretation but also the explanations offered in the statements themselves. He attacks the
statements as "unsubstantiated, self-exculpating claims" (534
n1) and Browning as gullible enough to fall for them. It is
noteworthy that a considerable part of Goldhagen's discussion
of factual evidence is given over to attacking Browning in
unusually strong language.* Why has Goldhagen concen-

---

* Taking issue with this statement, Goldhagen writes: "I do not say or imply
anything about [Browning's] integrity (*Goldhagen 1997*, 134). Yet consider this
passage: "Browning constantly plays up the reluctance and opposition of the men

trated on Police Battalion 101 when there are roughly one hundred and fifty investigations of other police battalions to choose from? While it would make sense in the context of a larger study to revisit this one case, it is peculiar to concentrate on the one case that has already been evaluated by a reputed historian.

In evaluating witness testimony, one can reject or view circumspectly all perpetrators' statements, particularly as to motive; they are, after all, a reflection of the perpetrators' self-image based on the desire for exculpation and tainted by retrospection. In doing so, however, one would lose one of the few possibilities available of gaining insight into the mentality of perpetrators, especially in those cases where a perpetrator feels compelled to unburden himself by confessing to his criminal acts and then tries to offer an explanation for his behavior. Nevertheless, wholesale rejection is a legitimate position. Goldhagen does not avail himself of this option though. He seems to follow no stringent methodological approach whatsoever. This is the problem. He prefers instead to use parts of the statements selectively, to reinterpret them according to his own point of view, or to take them out of context and make them fit into his own interpretative framework.

One example cited by Goldhagen is a letter by a captain in Battalion 101, which he considers of the greatest importance: "This one letter provides more insight," writes Goldhagen, "than do reams of the perpetrators' self-serving postwar testi-

---

which he manages to read into the material" (551, n65). Pursuing this style of argumentation in *The New Republic,* Goldhagen writes: "Some examples of this include the frequently invoked 'peer-pressure' explanation, for which even Christopher Browning, its champion, fails to present any actual evidence. He constructs it out of thin air" (23 December 1996). Many reviewers have deplored Goldhagen's attacks on Browning. Indeed Goldhagen himself refers to "this now oft repeated fiction that I have been unfair to Browning."

mony" (3–4, 382). The captain complains to his superiors about having to sign a declaration not to plunder. Goldhagen depicts this as significant proof that Germans had a scale of values and were able to make moral choices. However, when one examines this letter in the context of his other correspondence, the captain is revealed to be a malcontent, who regularly wrote letters to his superior. This letter has no great significance.[6]

Another example of Goldhagen's handling of the evidence is his description of an incident in which one of the officers brought his new bride to a ghetto-clearing and mass execution, angering many of the battalion members.[7] Trapp, the battalion commander, reprimanded this behavior publicly. Goldhagen interprets this as merely "a sense of chivalry" (242) and concern for "her welfare" (242), because the woman was pregnant. He also insinuates that wives "participated" (241) rather than simply being spectators of mass murder, which they were occasionally. Later on in the book, the whole incident is generalized (267, 378) as a representation of the fact that perpetrators routinely shared their murderous experiences with their wives. This generalization rests on a very small foundation of evidence and totally disregards the many examples of strict separation by the perpetrators of their "home life" from their life in "the East." This, by the way, led presumably to the disproportionally high number of divorces among perpetrators immediately after the war.

Expressions of shame and disapproval in the statements, if

---

6. ZStL, 208 AR-Z 27/62, III, 379–412. Goldhagen also depicts the content of the letter wrongly.

7. ZStL, 208 AR-Z 27/62 V, 1031–8, F.B.; VI, 1359–68, F.B.; VII, 1493–6, H.E.; VIII c, indictment StA Hamburg 141 Js 1957/62, 430–47.

not rejected out of hand for methodological reasons (533 n74, in connection with Police Battalion 65), are discredited by Goldhagen as mere expressions of "visceral disgust" (541 n68) and not of "ethical or principled opposition" (541 n68). To see how this view is a misrepresentation and, thus, unacceptable, one need only refer to the statement of the medical orderly of Battalion 101. He is very open and forthright in his interrogation. He describes his feelings with respect to the killing of the sick in a ghetto hospital quite sincerely: "it was so repulsive/disgusting to me and I felt so terribly ashamed."[8]* While

---

8. ZStL, 208 AR-Z 27/62, V, 971–9, F.V.

* The full sentence in the original reads: *"Diese Handlungsweise hat mich derartig angeekelt und ich habe mich derartig geschaemt, dass ich mich sofort umdrehte und den Raum wieder verliess."* Goldhagen's translation reads: "This way of acting disgusted me to such an extent, and I was ashamed to such a degree, that I turned around at once and left the room again" (546, n16). According to Goldhagen, the words "this way of acting" demonstrate that F.V. did not disapprove of the killing itself, but only of the "wanton manner" in which it was executed (*Goldhagen 1997, 135*). The German word *Handlungsweise* can be translated as "manner of acting," "behavior," "conduct"; in this context "conduct" seems to be the most appropriate translation. Neither the expression itself nor anything in the statement suggests that F.V. only objected to the "wanton manner" of the killing, and not the killing itself. On the contrary, in the same paragraph as the above-cited quotation, F.V. refers to this specific killing as "the greatest atrocity" (*Das Grausamste*); he refers to the day's events (the "ghetto-clearing") as "acts of outrage" (*Gewalttaten*). It bears mentioning that, in the German legal system, statements are not reported verbatim (see pp. 106–7 above); accordingly, specific expressions must be interpreted within the context of the full testimony. One should not overinterpret some words or neglect their context. It does not appear that Goldhagen takes into account this requirement when adducing statements as evidence.

When reviewing F.V.'s full testimony, several other facts are noteworthy: as a medical orderly, he did not have to shoot; he recalls conversing with Jewish victims during the ghetto clearings, which suggests that he regarded them as human beings; he openly reported and condemned the killings; notwithstanding a mistake in the data on his personal papers giving him a perfect alibi, he admitted to his presence in the Jewish hospital, also avowing that he experienced shame. Nothing suggests disingenuousness or approval. Compare, however, these facts with Goldhagen's account of F.V.: "Note, though, that this man's shame resulted from 'this way of acting,' from the wantonness of his comrades, not from the killing itself, to which his presence was intended to contribute. He wanted them to kill in a manner befitting good, upstanding Germans" (546, n16).

the notion of "principled opposition" would make sense when, for instance, dealing with attitudes of the German civilian population, its heuristic value becomes questionable when dealing with a group who, after all, did participate in crimes and can hardly claim "opposition" of any kind. For an honest statement under similar circumstances, one should more likely turn to one of the tentative and groping explanations Browning analyzes, in which the person is very open about what he saw, using descriptions like "cruel" (*grausam*), "murder plain and simple" (*glatter Mord*), "blatant swinishness" (*ausgesprochene Schweinerei*), and also very candidly talks about his participation in it. At the same time he describes his frame of mind within the context of the war, i.e., that he could not even imagine refusing to obey an order.[9] There are even examples of expressions of shame and guilt coupled with self-incriminating statements. One such statement cited by Browning is, not surprisingly, ignored by Goldhagen.[10]

Using Goldhagen's method of handling evidence, one could easily find enough citations from the Ludwigsburg material to prove the exact opposite of what Goldhagen maintains.

---

9. ZStL, 208 AR-Z 27/62, VI, 1114–28, E.N.

10. " 'The shooting of the men was so repugnant to me that I missed the fourth man. It was simply no longer possible for me to aim accurately. I suddenly felt nauseous and ran away from the shooting site. I have expressed myself incorrectly just now. It was not that I could no longer aim accurately, rather that the fourth time I intentionally missed. I then ran into the woods, vomited and sat down against a tree. To make sure that no one was nearby, I called loudly into the woods, because I wanted to be alone. Today I can say that my nerves were totally finished. I think that I remained alone in the woods for some two to three hours.'

"Kastenbaum returned to the edge of the woods and rode an empty truck back to the marketplace. He suffered no consequences; his absence had gone unnoticed because the firing squads had been all mixed up and randomly assigned. He had come to make his statement, he explained to the investigating attorney, because he had had no peace since attempting to conceal the shooting action" (Browning, 67–8).

III.

Goldhagen uses the activities of Police Battalion 65 as another illustration of his theory that "the Germans" killed "any Jew whom they discovered" with neither "prompting nor permission" (194), because this reflected "their own inwardly held standards" and their "internalized . . . need to kill Jews" (193). As proof, he recounts a number of killings that are contained in the investigation report of a German prosecutor. A reading of this report in full, and not selectively as in Goldhagen's case, reveals that the activities of Police Battalion 65 mirror the course of the German occupation policy; they implemented whatever orders were given to them at a specific time and place. They killed Jews and Russians in Lithuania and Russia, Jews and Poles in Poland. They deported Jews from Denmark and, at the end of the war in northern Yugoslavia, they killed Yugoslavs.[11] The report does not support Goldhagen's interpretation that priority was given to the killing of Jews and that "every German was inquisitor, judge and executioner" (194).

Individual statements are treated with similar selectiveness. Goldhagen cites the account of one witness who describes how a person was beaten to death, just because the name Abraham appeared in his papers (532 n54).[12] This incident is mentioned on page 2 of the statement, and on pages 3–4, the brutal and sexually sadistic murder of a young girl by one of the officers is described in graphic detail, vividly illustrating the atmo-

---

11. ZStL, 206 AR-Z 6/62, VIII, *Einstellungsverfuegung,* 2073–97.
12. ZStL, 206 AR-Z 6/62, III, 782–5, E.L.

sphere prevalent in Russia. Goldhagen makes no reference to it. The victim was not Jewish.

Goldhagen describes the activities of Police Battalion 309 in June 1941 in Bialystok (188–91) as ". . . the emblematic killing operation of the formal genocide" (191). He maintains that the battalion knew of the planned destruction of the Jews before its entry into the Soviet Union. (For a number of years, the majority of Holocaust scholars has endorsed the view that initially an order was given to kill Jewish men and Soviet functionaries, which was enlarged after roughly two months to a general killing order, including women and children.) Consequently, upon entering Bialystok "these Germans could finally unleash themselves without restraint upon the Jews" (188), and the whole battalion without any prompting "became instantaneous *Weltanschauungskrieger* or ideological warriors" (190). The Jewish quarters were searched, accompanied by many acts of cruelty, the Jewish population was herded into the marketplace, many were forced into the synagogue, and there burned alive.

Detailed examination of the statements themselves modifies this one-dimensional picture and shows Goldhagen's conclusions to be without foundation. Goldhagen stresses the importance of the extermination order and attacks Browning for having failed to mention it (529–30 n22). However, while some former members of the battalion confirm its existence,[13] others give differing statements, among them the clerk (Schreiber) through whose hands the orders would have had to pass.[14] One battalion member changes his story radically in a

---

13. ZStL, 205 AR-Z 20/60, V, 1339 rs, A.A.; VI, 1416, J.B.; 202 AR 2701/65, I, 95–6, H.G.

14. ZStL, 205 AR-Z 20/60, I, 289–90, G.E.; see IV, 1115–6 and IX, indictment StA Dortmund 45 Js 21/61, 2303, H. Sch.; III, 681 and VII, 1926 rs., R-J.B.; II, 485–6, E.O.; II, 514, T.D.

series of statements, and he speaks of an order to kill all Jews in his final statement only, the one that Goldhagen relies upon.[15] This should arouse the suspicion of a researcher. Closer scrutiny reveals the likely reason for the change of story: the defense strategy of the main defendants. As soon as the investigation commenced, intensive communication between former battalion members took place.[16] Two defense strategies emerged: to suggest a superior order in support of "military necessity" and to shift blame to the commander, who died during the investigation. This conclusion is corroborated by investigations of two battalions of the "Polizei Regiment Mitte" that, by the end of July 1941, still murdered male Jews only.[17]

The incident described by Goldhagen seems to have been in the nature of a pogrom, caused by a group of officers who, through their proximity to the SS, were ideologically zealous.[18] This is corroborated by two men from the rank and file who say that they were hustled into the action before they knew what was happening to them.[19] One describes how he was disgusted by the burning alive of defenseless people in the synagogue. Since both men confess, their testimony should carry great weight. While Goldhagen only speaks of "the Germans," the perpetrators in this case can be specifically identified. Of the fourteen main perpetrators who stood trial,

---

15. ZStL, 205 AR-Z 20/60, III, 764 (1963); XII, 2794–5 (1965); VII, 1813 rs (1966), E.M.

16. ZStL, 205 AR-Z 20/60, I, 73–7, M.R.; 78, letter E.W.; 177–93, E.W.; II, 459–62, H.Sch.; see Heiner Lichtenstein, *Himmlers gruene Helfer. Die Schutz- und Ordnungspolizei im "Dritten Reich"* (Koeln, 1990), 86–8. This has happened in other cases concerning Order Police.

17. Police Battalions 316 and 322, see ZStL SA 387, verdict LG Bochum 15 Ks 1/66 and SA 133, verdict LG Freiburg 1 Ks 1/63.

18. ZStL, 205 AR-Z 20/60, V, 1217–20, H.B.; II, 374, A.O.; II, 465–73, H. Sch.; V, 1343–4, J.O.; SA 214, verdict LG Wuppertal 12 Ks 1/67, 60–5.

19. ZStL, 205 AR-Z 20/60, III, 788–92, R.I. and V, 1280–4, W.L.; IX, 2327–33, indictment StA Dortmund 45 Js 21/61.

thirteen were career police officers and one came via the Waffen-SS; eight were party members.[20] One of the two company leaders had been involved, after World War I, with right-wing groups such as the "Freikorps" while the other was an SS member in 1933. They can hardly be considered "ordinary Germans."

The inadequacy of conclusions that are reached without a comparative approach is clearly illustrated by Goldhagen's discussion of the decision-making process within the phenomenon of the Holocaust. The lack of a comparative approach also undermines Goldhagen's own warning about the uncritical use of sources. He is not adverse to using exculpatory statements if it suits his line of argument. Goldhagen, as mentioned above, supports the older view that a general order was given to the Operational Task Forces (Einsatzgruppen) before they set out. His argument, though, is not up to the present level of the international debate on the subject. He bases his opinion mainly on two statements made by former commanders of Einsatzkommandos, Blume (149) and Filbert (149), which he proposes as "conclusive evidence" (153). Blume stood trial in Nuremberg, and he was part of a defense strategy organized by Otto Ohlendorf that had as its purpose to prove the existence of an alleged order by Hitler before the murder commenced. The presence of this order was intended to provide the keystone of a defense focused on superior orders as an excuse. Alfred Streim has demonstrated the existence of such a strategy by means of a painstaking and thorough analysis of the wide range of statements available. He has also shown how statements by the same person could change sub-

---

20. ZStL, 205 AR-Z 20/60, IX, indictment StA Dortmund 45 Js 21/61; SA 214, verdict LG Wuppertal 12 Ks 1/67, 8, ad R-J.B.

stantially over time. The Blume and Filbert statements are examples of this change.[21] Goldhagen, in his account, accepts uncritically the Ohlendorf line; he wrote a paper on Ohlendorf for his undergraduate degree. Goldhagen habitually dismisses as inadequate the works of the most respected scholars of the Holocaust, yet refers repeatedly to his own B.A. work (583 n45). The most telling example of the uncritical use of sources is what Goldhagen announces as perhaps "the most significant and illuminating testimony given after the war" (393). This testimony corroborates, according to him, that the perpetrators were genuinely motivated by "demonological hatred" against all Jews. The testimony is given by R. Maurach in defense of Ohlendorf in Nuremberg. Again, the best line of defense available, in the face of the indisputable number of murders committed by Einsatzgruppe D, was to claim orders from above and sincere ideological convictions. This, however, does not make this defense, which was rejected at Nuremberg, conclusive proof, the one argument "leaving us no choice but to adopt it" (583 n46).* In general, Goldhagen seems to have

---

21. Alfred Streim, *Die Behandlung sowjetischer Kriegsgefangener im Fall "Barbarossa"* (Heidelberg, 1981); Alfred Streim, *The Task of the SS Einsatzgruppen,* vol. iv (1987); Alfred Streim, *Reply to Helmut Krausnick,* vol. vi (1989), both: *Simon Wiesenthal Center Annual.*

* Goldhagen observes that he only once quoted his own undergraduate thesis, "which happens to be the only work of some length, of which I know, on the important figure of Otto Ohlendorf" (*Goldhagen 1997, 137*). He does, however, refer several times to Otto Ohlendorf, his trial at Nuremberg, and the decision-making process leading to the Holocaust (149, 153, 393–4, 401). His treatment of these matters is naive and does not meet accepted scholarly standards. One glance at a publication of the above-mentioned Maurach, for instance, shows him to be a German nationalist, very much on the political right, whose words should be considered with critical distance (cf. Reinhart Maurach, *Die Kriegsverbrecherprozesse gegen deutsche Gefangene in der Sowjetunion* [Muenchen, 1950]). An undergraduate who does not examine the writings of a figure he deems key (Maurach's "may be the most significant and illuminating testimony") can be excused; a doctoral candidate should have identified and corrected this problem. A thorough

difficulty comprehending that when perpetrators claim to have been motivated by Nazi propaganda, it need not be sincere; it can be a subterfuge or a very psychologically plausible line of self-exculpation. It attempts to supply "idealistic" motives for crimes committed.

IV.

In general terms, Goldhagen's descriptions of the activities of these police battalions entirely ignore the fact that the police units, rather than suddenly becoming "instantaneous *Weltanschauungskrieger*," had operated and conducted killings for some time in Poland, or other areas, before being sent to the Soviet Union. This neglect also applies to the examples he uses.[22] A police environment has a specific culture that is particularly manifest in a paramilitaristic setting, but Goldhagen entirely omits the factual, social, and historical context in which these policemen operated. Consider Goldhagen's attack on Browning for accepting the perpetrators' explanation of not wanting to appear cowardly if they refused the order to shoot. Goldhagen overlooks entirely the scale of values and perceptions of manly behavior prevalent in these particular settings. It might be disturbing that somebody would shoot children because he did not want to "appear soft," as expressed in a statement, but it captures something of the atmosphere of the time.[23] The framework of permissible action delineated by war

---

discussion of the testimonies of Einsatzgruppen personnel in respect to the question of the decision-making process can be found in Ralf Ogorreck, *Die Einsatzgruppen und die "Genesis der Endloesung"* (Berlin, 1996).

22. For instance, Battalion 309: see ZStL, 205 AR-Z 20/60, II, 462–4, H.Sch. and 482–4, E.O.

23. Ernst Klee, Willi Dressen, Volker Riess (eds.), *Schoene Zeiten* (Frankfurt, 1988), 81–3.

and occupation is neglected in the same way. Failing to refuse a given order is imperceptibly changed into an entirely voluntarist act of Jew-killing. Examples of the voluntary killing of Jews do, of course, exist, but they are not to be seen in the cases to which Goldhagen refers.

The most severe shortcoming of Goldhagen's treatment of the Order Police is that he analyzes activities outside of their proper historical and institutional context. In his introductory description of the Order Police, cited above, he states that police battalions are "most intimately involved in the genocide" (181). How is this a given? A more plausible argument with respect to this can be made for the smaller units of the Order Police, stationed all over the occupied East. They were involved in every step of the ghettoization, exploitation, and, finally, murder of the Jewish population over a prolonged period of time. They might have known the victims; they witnessed every detail of the Holocaust. In contrast, mobile units like the police battalions only sporadically moved into a particular region for mass killings. So why not choose the smaller units instead? If he had used stationary police units as his defining example, his hypothesis would have been devoid of any real content.

The Order Police in the Second World War grew enormously. The shortage of German personnel prevented effective policing of the occupied East. Non-German police forces had to be used to a great degree. The ratio of Germans to non-Germans ranged from between 1:10 to 1:50; in some places it was even higher. The majority were incorporated into the structural organization of the Order Police. In practical terms, the dispersion of limited resources meant that any rural police post would have been manned by a few German and a much larger group of non-German policemen. All of them took part in the persecution of Jews. Goldhagen would have had to address the question of what differences are to be seen in their respective behavior. And the same question can be asked of the police battalions themselves. "Schutzmannschaften," comprised of non-Germans, had been set up and were assigned the same functions as the German units. For example, Police Battalion 11, mentioned by Goldhagen in connection with its murderous activities in Belorussia in the fall of 1941 (271), was augmented by the Lithuanian "Schutzmannschaftsbataillon 2/12," manned by Lithuanian volunteers.[24] Germans and Lithuanians rotated in the killing actions—two companies were shooting while two were guarding. A number of statements of a type Goldhagen habitually accepts (though one might have reservations about such denunciatory statements), refer to the Lithuanians' particular bloodthirstiness.[25] Does this mean that Goldhagen's theory of the cognitive models of Germany's eliminationist anti-Semitic culture applies to Lithuanian cognitive models as well?

V.

The second empirical basis of Goldhagen's argument is the fact that Jews were used as forced labor. This part of his book he considers to be the "toughest test" of his hypothesis (465). He studies conditions in Jewish work camps, using concrete examples of two camps in Lublin: the Lipowa camp and the "Flughafen" camp. The many acts of cruelty and torture to which inmates were subjected are described in great detail.

---

24. ZStL, SA 119, indictment StA Kassel 31 Js 27/60, 14–17; Report of the investigations of war criminals in Australia, edited by the Attorney General's Department, Canberra (1993), 124–9.
25. StA Kassel 3a Ks 1/61, F.W.; E.B.

Goldhagen sees the economic irrationality of these conditions as a crucial feature. "Why did the Germans put Jews to work?" (283), he asks. "Why did they not simply kill them?" (283). The answer he gives is that the German "cognitive model of Jews" (285), which was "ingrained in German culture" (320), did not allow for Jewish work to be rationally motivated but only allowed such work to have "a symbolic and moral dimension" (285). The view expressed by Hitler, namely, that Jews are "lazy" and "parasites," is taken as "the common view in Germany." This collective view "echoed Hitler's" (285) own and led to the wish to make Jews suffer. "Germans derived emotional satisfaction" from putting Jews to work (284). They enjoyed the "production of Jewish misery" (320), even if it was economically counterproductive. "Jewish 'work' was not work . . . but a suspended form of death—in other words, it was death itself" (323).

Though not without a certain explanatory potential, Goldhagen's concept of the use of work to inflict gratuitous suffering on a doomed population is vitiated by the examples he cites. The work camps he describes were operating in 1942–43. At that time, the genocide, i.e., the overall plan to murder the Jewish population of Europe, had been in effect for two years. The idea of making Jews work was not a change in plans but rather a side issue, born out of the idea of getting the most use of the victims before having them killed. These facts are set out in detail in Goldhagen's main source,[26] the prosecutor's report. The general, immutable plan in which forced labor occurred involved ultimate destruction. Therefore, Goldhagen's comparison of the Lublin work camps with slave labor programs is nonsensical. Slave labor of Polish or Russian

26. ZStL, 208 AR-Z 74/60, LIV. Secondary sources exist as well.

people was designed not to kill them but to utilize their work capacity, albeit under the harshest of conditions. Consequently, work conditions varied, in particular when individual laborers were working on German farms, where some of them were not treated too badly. To prove that Germans tortured only Jews, Goldhagen compares a German farmer treating a Polish forced laborer with some decency with camp guards' treatment of Jews slated for extermination (313ff.). This is clearly illogical. A more viable comparison to the situation of Slavic forced laborers would be with the situation of those Jews who were, in 1942–43, still within a German environment and doing forced labor.[27] To support his stance that "Germans were murderous and cruel towards Jewish workers, and murderous and cruel in ways they reserved especially for Jews" (315), Goldhagen depicts the conditions of Slavic forced laborers in somewhat too rosy a manner (314). For instance, he ignores the fact that Russian women were forced to abort their unborn children, or were killed when found to be pregnant, even when the pregnancy resulted from rape. He also overlooks the fact that millions of Soviet POWs were starved to death before the German authorities realized that they had a problem with a labor shortage.* These examples do not support the thesis that Germans dealt with everybody but Jews in a manner that was dictated by economic rationality.

––––––––––

27. In detail described in Victor Klemperer, *Ich will Zeugnis ablegen bis zum letzten* (Berlin, 1995), II, 21–48.

* Although Goldhagen does mention the death by starvation of Soviet POWs (290), he does not integrate this crucial fact into his analysis and maintains a one-dimensional view of the German rationale for "Jewish work." Indeed, in his review of Goldhagen's book, Dieter Pohl illustrates similarities in German policy toward Soviet POWs and Jews in the matter of slave labor (Dieter Pohl, "Die Holocaust-Forschung und Goldhagens Thesen," in *Vierteljahreshefte für Zeitgeschichte,* Heft 1, 1997, 23–4).

The appropriate comparisons for the conditions in the Lublin work camps are the conditions in other camps. Everything Goldhagen describes was a daily occurrence in every concentration camp (which, parenthetically, existed as of 1933, before and apart from the Nazi policy to kill every person just because they were Jewish): the endless roll calls during which inmates perished from excessive heat, excessive cold, cruel punishments, public hangings, senseless work that was only meant to exhaust, health care that was a means of expediting death, and the plethora of arbitrarily inflicted humiliations and tortures from guards. What Goldhagen describes as being inflicted by the "camp's ordinary Germans" (307) onto "Jews, and only for Jews" (313) reflects what really happened if one replaces "Germans" with "guards" and "Jews" with "inmates." Of course, the behavior of guards was a reflection of the hatred of Jews, which was at the center of Nazi beliefs, but it also reflects the multitude of other individual personalized hatreds. Jews were very often the object of the cruelty of guards, but so were homosexuals, people wearing glasses, intellectuals, people with a disability, overweight people, and people who offered any type of resistance.

The commander of the "Flughafenlager" in 1942–43 was Christian Wirth and the majority of guards were his men. Wirth, who started out as a career police officer, was, from 1939–40 on, one of the central figures in the "Euthanasia" program, in which mental patients were killed. He moved on to the Lublin district where he was instrumental in setting up death camps. Wirth was an expert in the gassing of people. To refer to Christian Wirth and his subordinates as "the camp's ordinary Germans" (307) is misleading. In the same vein, the guards in the "Lipowa" camp, who are referred to as "an unextraordinary lot" (299), were three quarters SS men, hardened in camp duty.[28] In contrast to the behavior of these men, a group of fifteen employees of the SS company in charge of production in the camp are depicted by all victims as essentially harmless.[29] Goldhagen cannot have missed this telling juxtaposition; he cites the prosecutor's report in the middle of the page after these facts are set out. How does this fit into Goldhagen's claim that "postwar testimony . . . reveals little consciousness of differences in attitude or action between those who were either Party or SS members and those who were not" (274)?

One additional point should be made in connection with Goldhagen's description of the Lublin work camps. An all too common feature of his discussion is the use of nearly malicious language for the description of particularly terrible facts, presumably to convey sarcastic detachment. It is wholly undignified. A reader can conclude for him- or herself that the murder of forty thousand people within a few days is an enormous crime and that the code name "Action Harvest Festival" is a travesty, without being told by the author that this was "aptly named in keeping with the Germans' customary love of irony" (291)—to name only one of many examples.

VI.

The third empirically based section of this book deals with "death marches." One march, from the Helmbrechts camp, is described in detail. A group of Jewish female inmates were

---

28. ZStL, 208 AR-Z 74/60, XLVI, 8400–12, *Aktenvermerk.*
29. ZStL, 208 AR-Z 74/60, XLVI, 8441–42, *Aktenvermerk.*

taken on foot, accompanied by male and female guards, through the border area of Germany and Czechoslovakia. No contextual framework for these events is provided; the events are merely told in a narrative style. Conditions on the march were terrible, as they had been in the camp. The Jewish women were already emaciated and starving, food and shelter were denied them, and they were relentlessly forced to continue marching. A number of them were killed during the march. Even after an explicit order by Himmler to refrain from killing, the murder continued.

Supported by a few similar examples from other death marches, Goldhagen arrives at a general explanation. This irrational, extremely cruel behavior by "ordinary Germans," directed exclusively against Jews, is proof of the demonological, undying hatred of "Germans" against "Jews." "To the very end, the ordinary Germans . . . willfully, faithfully and zealously slaughtered Jews" (371). He argues that, in this situation, the behavior of the German guards was entirely irrational, since Germany had already been defeated. He posits that the only reasonable thing in the circumstances would have been a change in behavior and that the reason for a continuation of the killing must reside in deeper irrational urges.

Goldhagen's account of the death marches is extremely distorted. In consulting the secondary sources he cites, we quickly encounter a number of facts that contradict the picture he draws. Krakowski, for instance, relates the fact that there were Jewish and non-Jewish inmates on death marches and gives detailed breakdowns of the percentages of each group on the marches he mentions. In the period of March–April 1945, in which the Helmbrechts march took place, Krakowski estimates that 250,000 prisoners were forced to take part in marches, two thirds of whom were not Jewish.[30]* Other examples, not cited by Goldhagen, show that conditions on all of these marches were very similar, including those with only non-Jewish inmates.[31]

When compared with investigations of other death marches, one finds that the range of behavior patterns is much wider than that suggested by Goldhagen. One can find examples for almost any attitude on the part of the guards, ranging from extreme cruelty to what might be considered its opposite, and, also to some degree, of the two attitudes coexisting.[32] On an individual basis, guards behaved quite differently from each other, reflecting their own degree of identification with camp behavior. This is reported to be the case in the Helmbrechts march, although Goldhagen does not mention it.[33] The same

---

30. Shmuel Krakowski, "The Death Marches in the Period of the Evacuation of the Camps," in *The Nazi Concentration Camps* (Jerusalem, 1984), 482; Krakowski, "Death Marches," in *Encyclopedia of the Holocaust.*

* To be sure, Goldhagen, in referring to the prisoners on the death marches, says: "Many of these were non-Jews, since not only Jews inhabited the concentration camp system." His footnote to this sentence reads: "The majority of them were, however, Jews," based on a Czechoslovak publication from 1965. Goldhagen continues: "Nevertheless, the evidence suggests that the mortality rate of Jews in this final period of destruction was, as in the camps themselves, significantly higher than that of non-Jews" (330). However, as mentioned above, Krakowski supplies precise figures, not an indeterminate "many." In the German edition of the *Encyclopedia of the Holocaust,* Krakowski explicitly states that in the final phase there was no difference in the treatment of Jews and non-Jews after November 1944 (see Krakowski, "Todesmaersche" in *Enzyklopaedia des Holocaust. Die Verfolgung und Ermordung der europaeischen Juden,* Band III, Muenchen 1995, 1412–1416: *"Die Juden wurden bei den anhaltenden 'Evakuierungen' ebenso behandelt wie die anderen Haeftlinge"*). According to Dieter Pohl, the victims of one particularly gruesome massacre in Gardelegen, which Goldhagen describes, were mostly non-Jewish Poles (Pohl, op. cit., 35).

31. See, for instance, the death march from Wiener-Neudorf, where no Jews were present, Bertrand Perz, "Der Todesmarsch von Wiener Neudorf nach Mauthausen. Eine Dokumentation," in DOW *Jahrbuch* 1989, 117–37.

32. Perz, "Der Todesmarsch," 117–37.

33. ZStL, SA 343, verdict LG Hof Ks 7/68, 82; see 58–9 and 210.

diversity of behavior can be observed in the civilian population. In the Helmbrechts march, the German population seems to have been supportive of the victims, offering food and shelter, but all succor was forbidden and thwarted by the guards.[34]* One also finds entirely different behavior, like the sudden outbursts of animosity and violence toward the miserable marchers, who were already in a desolate condition.[35]

---

34. ZStL, SA 343, verdict LG Hof Ks 7/68, 57–9, 82–3, 194–5, and 210.

* At the time I wrote the review, the Helmbrechts investigation had resumed and the file was closed to scholars. In the meantime, it has been reopened, and my new research enables me to be more extensive in my commentary on Goldhagen's text. The inmate contingent that initially left KL Helmbrechts consisted half of Jewish and half of non-Jewish inmates. On the fifth day, they reached another sub-camp of KL Flossenbuerg, where the marching columns were reorganized, Jews were separated from non-Jews, and for the rest of the way, apart from a small group, there were only Jewish female prisoners on the death march. In the indictment and the verdict, the crimes committed on every day of the march are carefully listed. Therefore, one can easily compare the first part of the death march (mixed prisoners) with the second part (almost exclusively Jewish prisoners). Such a juxtaposition reveals no fundamental difference in the behavior of the guards. This is diametrically opposed to Goldhagen's conclusion: "The Helmbrechts march turned out to be a death march for Jews and only for Jews" (346).

The investigation reveals other important facts that contradict Goldhagen's assertions. First, of the twenty-two camp guards, seven were from Hungary/ Romania. (At this late stage of the war, up to 70 percent of camp guards were not "*Reichsdeutsche*," that is, from Germany proper.) It is reported by the victims that three particularly notorious shooters and sadists at Helmbrechts belonged to the group of non-German guards. While the fact is referred to by Goldhagen, its logical consequences are not reflected in his analysis, perhaps because it is hardly reconcilable with his theory of the cognitive models caused by centuries of German history and socialization.

Second, many statements recall as particularly horrific the protracted and gruesome torture to death in open view of a Russian camp doctor who had attempted to escape. The victim was from Kiev, the perpetrator from Stryj in Galicia. How does this square with Goldhagen's statement: "The Germans' torturing and killing was not diffuse, their actions were not the expressions of sadistic or generally brutalized personalities, that seek gratification on any potential victim. Their cruelty and lust to kill was victim specific, reserved and centered upon the Jews. They chose to torture and kill only when they had Jewish victims" (357)?

35. As examples of both types of behavior: Solly Ganor, "Der Todesmarsch," in *Dachauer Hefte* 11, 1995; Peter Sturm, Evakuierung, in *Dachauer Hefte* 11, 1995; Verdict LG Marburg 6 Ks 1/68, ZStL, SA 386; Indictment StA Hannover 11Js 5/73, ZStL, SA 503, Verdict LG Hannover 11 Ks 1/77, ZStL, SA 503.

A comparative perspective casts further doubt on Goldhagen's notion that the only rational behavior for the guards, in the shadow of the imminent defeat of Germany, would have been to either release the inmates or treat them humanely. The extensive materials on crimes committed in the last weeks of the war[36] show numerous instances when the police, SS, and German army members turned, in a rabid and destructive way, not against Jews, but against the German population itself, i.e., against whomever was showing signs of *"defaitisme."* Hitler's own response to the certainty of defeat was the wish to see the German population destroyed. In this period of chaos and destruction, human behavior did not seem to conform to what Goldhagen describes as being the only "rational" way.

VII.

Thus far, a close review of Goldhagen's evidentiary base has shown the selective way in which he has interpreted his sources. On a larger scale, the greatest shortcoming of the book is that he uses such a small sample of the investigations and sources available. He takes selected parts and blows them up out of proportion. Sweeping generalizations then emerge from these distortions, like an image reflected by a magnifying mirror. Had he used a broader source base and applied the comparative method, a truer picture would have emerged. In the last part of the book, there is a brief section headed "comparative perspective" (406). But it does not serve the purpose

---

36. Available in published form, for instance, in the edition of German verdicts by Rüters, also in numerous printed works.

of making any real comparisons, as Goldhagen only brushes the whole issue aside by applying his own style of argument and logic. He starts out with a question: Could we conceive of Danes and Italians committing the Holocaust? This is a biased rhetorical question since these are the two generally known examples of groups who did not participate in the genocide. So why ask the question? Danes, for example, were not enlisted in any of the units that committed mass murder, so how can they be used as a comparison?

Goldhagen's theory of the motivation of perpetrators is flawed by the absence of any comparison between a German and non-German perpetrator. As mentioned above, the contribution of non-Germans to policing Eastern Europe was substantial, and policing in the context of German occupational policies included involvement in crimes. Did their behavior differ? And if so, in what way? For Eastern Europe, comparisons would have been easy to make since Germans and non-Germans were working side by side in police units and police posts. Comparisons with collaborating police forces, such as the French, or with allies like the Croatian or Hungarian police might have been more complex.

A classic example of non-Germans who fit the picture Goldhagen wishes to paint of Germans is the "Arajs Kommando." Named after their leader, Viktor Arajs, this was a group composed of Latvian men, mainly students or former army officers, with right-wing political backgrounds. Within days of the arrival of the German forces in Riga, Arajs made contact with the leader of Einsatzgruppe A, Walter Stahlecker, and offered his services. In the following months, his group, officially known as the "Latvian Auxiliary Security Police," did nothing but kill Jews. They were active in Riga and moved around all of Latvia; parts of the group were sent to

Belorussia. The guards in camps located in Latvia were Arajs Kommando members. The killing actions were extremely gruesome, with the perpetrators literally wading in blood, getting drunk during the killing, and afterwards participating in large celebrations. Survivor accounts describe the terrible conditions in the basement of the Kommando headquarters where Jews were kept. There they were tortured, degraded, and raped. All of the Arajs Kommando members were volunteers. They were free to leave at any time.[37] Goldhagen offers evasive explanations for non-German perpetrators: "The Germans had defeated, repressed and dehumanized Ukrainians, and there were pressures operating on the Ukrainians that did not exist for the Germans" (408–9). He also states that the "Germans' conduct towards their eastern European minions . . . was generally draconian" (409). Apart from smacking considerably of standard revisionism, these assumptions certainly do not apply to the Arajs Kommando. All the "typical German" patterns of behavior like "rage, a lust for vengeance, that unleashed the unprecedented cruelty" (414) were present here as well. How does this fit into Goldhagen's explanatory framework?

Admittedly, the Arajs Kommando is an extreme case, but it is by no means an isolated one. Many similar examples exist. Camps in the occupied Soviet Union were run with a minimum of German personnel. The Koldyczewo camp, north of Baranowice in Belorussia, for instance, was run by one German.[38] All the other guards were non-German. The camp was operated in the same way as all camps; inmates were tortured and worked to death and large killing actions were conducted.

---

37. StA Hamburg 141 Js 534/60, ZStL, 207 AR-Z 7/59.
38. ZSt Dortmund 45 Js 19/64, ZStL, 202 AR-Z 94/59.

A great number of camps in Soviet territory functioned without German personnel at all and with only minimal supervision. How does this fit into the notion of the "camp system" being the German "society's emblematic institution" (459) and the view of a potential "Germanic Europe, which essentially would have become a large concentration camp, with the German people as its guards" (459)?

To forestall possible misinterpretation, all of the foregoing certainly resulted from German policies. Orders for Koldyczewo, for instance, were received from the Security Police in Baranowice. The introduction of a comparison with non-German perpetrators does not take anything away from the overall responsibility of Germany for the Second World War and the Holocaust. But it is certainly highly relevant to the question of individual motivation and its root causes.

Goldhagen studiously avoids putting his theory to such a comparative test. Even though it is evident from the footnotes that he is familiar with the investigation of the Arajs Kommando and other similarly telling cases, these facts are never mentioned. He simply dismisses comparisons as irrelevant since the Germans were "the central and only indispensable perpetrators of the Holocaust" (409). This tactic allows him to analyze the motivation of the German perpetrators while excluding a comparison that would have revealed the falseness of his conclusions and, thus, would have denied him the authority to conclude that all this was specifically an expression of the German national character. He further postulates that any research on the behavior of non-Germans, if it were to be undertaken, would only serve as an illumination of the Germans' actions, because only Germans were "the prime movers" (409). According to him, this research would not change his results. An argument of immaculate circularity.

Germany was certainly responsible for the Holocaust and it is also clear that Viktor Arajs became a mass murderer only because of the overall German plan to destroy the Jewish population of Latvia. Yet Goldhagen's procedural negligence, which results in false conclusions, is evident with respect to the policemen in Police Battalion 101 and all other examples discussed in the book. None of the people discussed in Goldhagen's three case studies was making policy; they all responded, at least initially, to a given political situation. The question of the overall political and moral responsibility, which lies with Germany, is not a relevant consideration when examining the personal response and motivation of the individual low-level perpetrator.*

VIII.

In light of his circumscribed and biased use of archival sources, it is perhaps not surprising that Goldhagen is also highly selective in his use of secondary literature. Early on in the book, he provides an overview of German history from the Middle Ages to the Second World War, basing his narrative entirely on secondary sources. As the main facts of German

---

* To clarify my argument, a comparison between Germans and non-Germans belonging to the same category of perpetrator is needed before one can draw conclusions about German-specific behavior. Goldhagen's argument that such a comparison would not be enlightening inasmuch as the Germans made the high level political decisions (*Goldhagen 1997,* 147) is unconvincing and of questionable relevance to conclusions that are based on an analysis of low-level perpetrators. For each of the three groups of perpetrators Goldhagen uses as examples—members of police battalions, camp guards in Lublin and in Helmbrechts—comparisons between Germans and non-Germans should and could have been attempted before reaching conclusions about motivation, particularly when expressed as specific to a national group.

history are widely known, it does not seem worthwhile to devote too much time to a review of this part of the book. Suffice it to say that Goldhagen produces a tunnel-vision view of "this pre-Holocaust age" (70), which leaves no room for either historical context or a comparative framework. He posits an unbroken continuity in Germany from the anti-Judaism of the Christian churches in the Middle Ages to the racial anti-Semitism of the nineteenth and twentieth centuries, in which Jews were seen as "a binary opposite of the German" (55). Consequently, German history appears as one great endless struggle of the Germans against the Jews, regardless of the context. When the Nazis were "elected to power" (*sic*) (419), the teleology of German history fulfilled itself. Needless to say, in order to support this view, Goldhagen substantially manipulates the secondary sources he uses.

Goldhagen eliminates the political context of the Nazi movement and ignores the fact that the Nazi regime was a repressive system from the start. He makes no reference to the fact that the Nazis were a right-wing party, promoting conservative and right-wing political views (some of which turn up in the creeds of right-wing movements to this day). Indeed, by playing down all political factors, such as the struggle between left and right in the Weimar Republic and the Nazis' suppression of all left-wing groups and the labor movement, Goldhagen is able to make statements like "the Nazi German revolution was, on the whole, consensual"; "a peaceful revolution . . . the repression of the political left in the first years notwithstanding" (456). This approach beautifies the realities of the Nazi regime to an uncomfortable extent.

The important questions—How widespread and deeply rooted was anti-Semitism? To what extent did the German population support the Nazis' anti-Semitic measures? And how exactly did the persecution of the Jews affect Hitler's and the Nazis' popularity?—are certainly not resolved. Goldhagen does not contribute to the debate.

IX.

Goldhagen's book is not driven by sources, be they primary or secondary. He does not allow the witness statements he uses to speak for themselves; he uses source material only as an underpinning for his preconceived theory. Rather the book is driven by the author's choice of language, and it can only be understood by analyzing those choices and his generally argumentative style. Verbosity and repetitiveness are the book's most striking features.

Discursive Techniques

Goldhagen uses several techniques to transform his assumptions into what he describes as the "unassailable truth." In particular, the introductory and concluding chapters are full of examples, of which a few must be demonstrated in detail. One is to use a single fact to support an overall generalization. For instance, a protest letter by Pastor Hochstaedter is described as being "all but singular" (433), a "tiny, brief flame of reason and humanity . . . flickering invisibly . . . in the vast antisemitic darkness that had descended upon Germany" (434). Goldhagen uses the letter as a foil to "cast into sharp relief" (431; a favorite expression of the author) the attitude of the Christian churches in general who did not object to the "Nazis' ferocious antisemitism" (435). They were eliminationist anti-Semitic themselves. Based on another single document taken entirely out of context,[39] he arrives at a sweeping conclusion that the churches gave "an ecclesiastical imprimatur of genocide" (433).*

A second technique is the application of a form of reasoning, which is boldly presented as common sense, and therefore as being the only logically possible explanation. Goldhagen maintains that the "indifference" of the "German people" (439) toward the fate of the Jews is a "psychologically implausible attitude" (440) since "people generally flee scenes and events that they consider to be horrific, criminal or dangerous" (440). Thus, since part of the German population watched the burning of synagogues in the November pogrom "with curiosity"—a modifier added by the author (440)—they were not indifferent but rather pitiless (440).

A third technique is a twisted manipulation of the interpretations of other scholars in order to provide foils for his own line of argument. This has already been demonstrated in a number of earlier examples. A particularly striking one is Goldhagen's discussion, and rejection, of what he calls "conventional explanations." One of these, according to the author, is the assumption that "the Germans were in principle opposed . . . to a genocidal program" (385). Raul Hilberg is depicted as "an exemplar of this sort of thinking" (385)

---

39. See *Kirchliches Jahrbuch für die Evangelische Kirche in Deutschland, 1933–1944* (Guetersloh, 1948).

* The source Goldhagen cites is a collection illustrating the various standpoints of the Protestant churches at the time, ranging from the most pro-Nazi to the most anti-Nazi. The proclamation quoted by Goldhagen reflects the position taken by the most pro-Nazi segment of the Protestant churches. Other church groups voiced their dissent, as shown in other documents reproduced in the same source. One would expect a scholar to reflect this, not to cite only the document that fits his theory.

because he contemplates the question of how the German bureaucracy overcame its moral scruples (385). After accusing Hilberg of heresy for assuming that "the German bureaucracy naturally had moral scruples" (385), Goldhagen rejects Hilberg's analysis on the basis that "explanations proceeding in this manner cannot account for Germans . . . volunteering for killing duty" (385)—which, of course, misses Hilberg's point entirely. In these passages, Hilberg is explicitly not dealing with men directly involved in the killing actions.

Another frequent tactic is the omission of a sufficient context or other possible evidence that might be contradictory. Goldhagen mentions celebrations at either the conclusion of large killing actions, as in Chelmno or in Stanislawo, or at a particular stage in the extermination program, as in Lublin after the fifty thousandth victim had been killed, at which the "Germans" "take joy, make merry and celebrate their genocide of the Jews" (453). He omits to mention that the same parties took place in "Euthanasia" institutions like Hadamar, to celebrate the ten thousandth corpse,[40] or, for that matter, in Grafeneck also.[41] The victims of the "Euthanasia" program were mostly Germans. While the available evidence suggests that a possible explanation for this behavior is to be found in the progressive brutalization of members in mass-killing institutions, it does not support Goldhagen's notion of "the transvaluated world of Germany during the Nazi period [where] ordinary Germans deemed the killing of Jews to be a beneficent act for humanity" (452–3). Goldhagen's crowning

---

40. ZStL, 439 AR 1261/68, *Sonderband* 19, S.2878–9, I.Sch.
41. Ernst Klee, *Dokumente zur "Euthanasie"* (Frankfurt, 1985), 119, ZStL, *Anlageband* 13 AR 179/65, *Vernehmungsprotokolle* GStA FfM Js 8/61 u. Js 7/63, G.S.

misrepresentation is the description of such a celebration in Cesis, Latvia: "On the occasion of their slaughter of the Jews of Cesis, the local German security police and members of the German military assembled to eat and drink at what they dubbed a 'death banquet [*Totenmahl*] for the Jews.' During their festivities, the celebrants drank repeated toasts to the extermination of the Jews" (453). Goldhagen fails to mention that Latvians and Germans were sitting down at the same table and that one local Latvian police officer instigated target practice at Jews in the course of the festivities. This was viewed with disgust by the German army officers.[42]

Finally, one can even find blatantly false renderings of original text, as when Goldhagen refers to a verse written by a member of Police Battalion 9, which was attached to Einsatzkommando 11a. He states that this member "managed to work into his verse, for the enjoyment of all, a reference to the 'skull-cracking blows' . . . that they had undoubtedly delivered with relish to their Jewish victims" (453). These words, found in a disgusting and anti-Semitic poem, refer however to "the cracking of nuts."[43]

The Creation of the "Ordinary German"

"Ordinary Germans" is one of the key terms of Goldhagen's book. It rests on the shaky empirical foundation of an evaluation of the social background of members of Police Battalion

---

42. ZStL, 207 AR-Z 22/70, *Sonderbaende* II, V.L. and III, R.K.; StA Luebeck 2 Js 394/70.

43. In German: *"Fernder* [sic] *die Juden und Krimtschaken/verlernen schnell das Nuessknacken,"* ZStL, 213 AR 1900/66, DokBd IV, 672–7. A rough translation is: "Also, the Jews and the Krimchaks will be quickly taught not to crack nuts." That is, they will no longer live a life of leisure and plenty.

101, and on the author's conclusion that the backgrounds of these members do not differ significantly from the social stratification of German society overall. As mentioned above, of the behavior of members of police units and the German population in general this equation is questionable since it ignores all concrete historical and institutional contexts. Moreover, Goldhagen does not test the evidence with comparisons to other police battalions because this would have yielded quite different results. Instead, he simply relies on the technique of greater and greater generalization to make his point.

Goldhagen's indiscriminate use of language is an essential part of his strategy. The term *ordinary German* is used everywhere. Concentration camp guards are "ordinary German women" (365); all perpetrators are "ordinary Germans" (371). It quickly becomes apparent that there is no sociological or factual meaning contained in the term. Consider a phrase like: "other ordinary Germans in the SS and the Party" (178). "Ordinary German" is nothing but an empty label if it can even be applied to the SS, who were at the forefront of the ideological movement.

The word *German,* both as a noun and an adjective, is used excessively throughout the book. This is entirely in keeping with the author's view that the specific traits of German culture are the root cause of the Holocaust. He states this right at the beginning of his book where he speaks of perpetrators "only in the understood context that these men and women were Germans first, and SS men, policemen, and camp guards second" (7, also 6). For Goldhagen, nationality is of the essence. Surprisingly, what is not of the essence is a person's actual activity or function. This is evident in the language he uses: *Concentration camp guard* becomes *German guard* and, then, *the Germans in the camps* (cf. 306, 307, 371). The actual function of the perpetrator in the commission of the crime has been eliminated. Only the nationality remains. Goldhagen even corrects supporting sources. For example, he quotes a passage from Chaim Kaplan's *Warsaw Diaries:* "The beast within the Nazi is whole, completely healthy—it attacks and preys upon others; but the man within him is pathologically ill. Nature has struck him with the illness of sadism, and this disease has penetrated into the very fibre of his being. There is no Nazi whose soul is not diseased, who is not tyrannical, sadistic" (397). Goldhagen, however, then adds in a footnote: "Kaplan's use of 'Nazis' should be read as 'Germans'" (583, n53). It should be noted that the same "logic" is not applied to every instance. Thus in the description of attacks on Jews in Vienna after the "Anschluss," Goldhagen quotes a source that uses the term *Nazis* for those who are torturing Jews but does not suggest changing it to *Austrians* (286–7). By the similarly excessive use of the adjective, for instance in the phrase "German culture of cruelty" (255), a further step is taken. It is not German nationals anymore who commit cruel acts, but cruelty itself become a German trait. "Cruelty" in the camps is "revealing of the Germans' state of mind" (308).

By this method of enlarging the meaning and use of the word *German,* Goldhagen is able to make the Holocaust a "German national project" (11). Finally, he combines the two methods. The genocide was committed by "Germans" with the Germans' "general propensity to violence" (568 n108) and all perpetrators were "ordinary Germans," meaning for the author "Germany's representative citizens" (456). He extends the inference to every other German: "the conclusion drawn about the overall character of the members' actions[44] can, indeed must, be generalized to *the German people in general.*

---

44. Of Police Battalion 101, RBB.

What these *ordinary* Germans did also could have been expected of other *ordinary* Germans" (402, emphasis in original).

Imagination

Goldhagen argues that a comprehensive picture of the normal lives of the perpetrators is needed to understand them fully, that they should be shown in every facet of their existence. Only such a "thick," "rather than the customary paper-thin description" (7) can explain their actions. One can only agree with this approach. Certainly, a more detailed and extensive description of perpetrators and, in particular, their mind-set at the time of committing their crimes than can be found in available historical literature would be of the greatest interest. Goldhagen claims to achieve what all previous studies have failed to do, namely, to integrate "the micro, meso and macro levels" of the individual with the "institutional and social context" (266).

For this purpose, Goldhagen examines a number of Daily Orders (*Tagesbefehle*) issued by the commander of the Order Police in Lublin in the years from 1942 to 1944. These Daily Orders outline the shape of the day. They announce time-tables, work tasks, ordinary events like sports activities or movies—whatever the commander wants to be made public. Nowhere do these documents convey the moods, emotions, and mind-set of the men to whom these orders were addressed. Around the fifteen orders he selected, Goldhagen weaves a web of fantasies about the "more conventional type of German cultural life" after the "slaughtering [of] unarmed Jews by the thousands" (263). He speculates on such questions as "how many of the killers discussed their genocidal activities . . . , when they went at night to their wives and girlfriends" (268), or "whether they might have seen the irony in the title of a play 'Man Without Heart' " (270).

Goldhagen has not one shred of a fact to rely on here. Everything is written in the "if" style used in bad historical novels. This is not true historical research.

The reason for the paucity of scholarly writing on the "thick lives" of perpetrators is not due to the lack of interest on the part of historians. Rather, it results from the lack of available material on which to base a study. Occasional finds in investigative files, for example, are so few and far between that the methodical research required would exceed the capacity of any researcher. Ordinarily, scholars accept the limitations imposed on them by the sources.

X.

Goldhagen started out his book with some fundamentally disturbing questions: Why do we believe that Germans are like us? Why do we believe Germany was "a 'normal' society . . . similar to our own" (15)? Why assume the " 'normalcy' of the German people" (31)? These remarks are made without any qualifiers as to a specific historical period. Goldhagen's recommendation is not to assume, but to review the Germans "with the critical eye of an anthropologist" (15), as if studying another species.

Goldhagen's book abounds with examples of his particular image of "the Germans." Suffice it to cite only a few here: the German is "generally brutal and murderous in the use of other peoples" (315), and is a "member of an extraordinary, lethal political culture" (456) whose cruelties stand out "in the long annals of human barbarism" (386). Similar expressions, as graphic as those cited, can be found on almost every page of the book, confirming Goldhagen's image of the counterspecies his anthropological view has detected. Goldhagen's book is based on his Ph.D. dissertation. Would someone receive a Ph.D. at Harvard who begins by posing the question whether blacks or women are human beings like "us"?

While the reader is not left in any doubt about "the Germans," the more interesting question remains: Who are the normal "we" referred to by Goldhagen in his book? The author never clarifies this explicitly. Instead, he offers his views on how people should normally react and hence how far outside normal human behavior the perpetrators were. Normal people "regard and respect" elders (189), feel "sympathy," pity (357), and the "instincts of nurturance" (201) toward sick people, toward undernourished people, toward people lying in an exhausted condition on the street. "After all, there is usually a natural flow of sympathy for people who suffer great wrongs" (441).

Goldhagen's concept of "natural" human behavior is striking. One glance at present-day American social realities should be enough to raise doubt as to whether sick and weak people necessarily arouse "instincts of nurturance." Goldhagen ignores the equally evident human potential for evil and destructiveness. He addresses this potential in a footnote (581 n25) but sees its acceptance as "cynicism." Hence he must attack any concepts that involve the allegedly " 'universal' psychological and social psychological factors" (390; see also 409). And in fact, he dismisses them as "abstract, ahistorical explanations . . . conceived in a social-psychological laboratory" (391; see also 389). Milgram's experiments on cruelty and obedience to authority are brushed aside as providing "untenable" (383) explanations.

By denying the possibility that the crimes committed during the Holocaust are within the scope of human behavior, he places these crimes and their perpetrators outside the realm of human possibility. Only the Germans could have behaved the way they did; nobody else. Their behavior is "unfathomable" and outside of "our" world. As a consequence, it cannot be repeated by someone else. The Holocaust is reduced to a specific historical event, outside of "our" world, separated from "us."

The same can be said of Goldhagen's description of anti-Semitism. He insists that it is divorced from any real historical or social framework. On this basis, he rejects explanations that equate economics or "scapegoat strategies" with motives (39, 44). In his view, anti-Semitism is divorced from reality; it is irrational, wild, and hallucinatory. It is outside the context of human interaction and outside the context of human reason. He argues that there is a "generally constant antisemitism becoming more or less manifest" (39) so that the observation of the decrease of anti-Semitism is not accurate. It represents a "diminution of antisemitic vituperation" (43) not "a decrease in antisemitic belief and feeling" (43), only "a differential expression" thereof (43). A true observation and appraisal of reality has become impossible.

The insistence with which Goldhagen promotes this theory—the word "must" is in constant use (see 392ff.)—shows the centrality of his argument. Anti-Semitism is a demonological, hallucinatory force, out of the reach of ordinary perception. Germans' crimes are outside the realm of human behavior. This extreme polarization has its consequences. In juxtaposition with the enormity of the injustice done to the Jews, other events take on a much more benign aspect. Jews are slaughtered while non-Jews are killed (195). Non-Jews in concentration camps live "a life of comparative luxury" (343) and enjoy "shocking longevity" (340). This is jarring. Worse still are the wider comparisons. In Soviet gulags, the "cruelty of the guards did not even begin to approach that which the Germans inflicted on the Jews" (587 n91). Goldhagen presumes to claim that other genocides were actually supported by rational motivation, including the Armenian genocide and the genocide between the Hutus and the Tutsis (412 n86, 587).

In Goldhagen's view, the Holocaust is both separated from what is considered normal human behavior and also demonstrates, from the perspective of today, a historical terminableness. Goldhagen's "we" could not have committed the indignities of the Holocaust, but even "the Germans" suddenly and drastically changed after the war. Here, Goldhagen's argumentation becomes almost farcical. After drawing the sinister picture of a nation that for centuries was in the grip of "demonological, hallucinatory antisemitism," of a people impregnated with vicious notions of Jews, he now proposes the unrealistic idea of a sudden behavioral change. The change is significantly due, according to him, to American reeducation efforts—the only time any historian has attributed real influence to this program (593–4 n53, 582 n38). Anybody who knows anything about the real Germany is aware, of course, that the reverse is true. Although Goldhagen's argument is illogical, its function is clear; the Holocaust is now firmly outside the realm of ordinary people's actions and it is over historically. The Holocaust is sanitized.

XI.

One of the most striking features of this book is the broad narrative style in which events are recounted. Goldhagen clearly states his reason for adopting this style, namely, to "eschew the clinical approach" (22). We should "describe for ourselves every gruesome image" (22) in order to better understand the reality of the Holocaust. In accordance with this aim, the author fills page after page with graphic descriptions of gruesome events during mass-murder actions and in camps.

Whether this is really the role of a scholar is doubtful. After all, there is an extensive collection of survivors' memoirs and testimonies, in which we can hear the voices of the victims themselves. In the approach Goldhagen advocates, the historian takes on the position of an intermediary who is not interpreting sources but retelling the events in the light of his own imagination. It's his voice we hear!

More than fifty years have passed since the end of the Second World War. The ranks of Holocaust survivors are getting thinner. More and more, the Holocaust is moving into the realm of interpreters, be they scholars or artists, or simply anyone making use of the lessons history teaches. This transition brings with it an obligation. We, i.e., people without direct personal involvement—be it as members of the second or third generation—have to resist both the temptation to assume the voice of survivors and the moral authority that goes with it. The Holocaust is the most morally explosive event in the Western world today. But its meaning is being diminished by constant trivialization. Everyone can observe daily, for him- or herself, how the terms of reference of the Holocaust are morally abused in political and public life; every abortion clinic is called an Auschwitz. There is no way to stop this process. The community of Holocaust scholars, however, is under a special obligation to counter the ongoing process of trivialization. Only by scrupulously differentiating between one's ego and the object of one's studies can the meaning of the Holocaust be preserved and protected.

Goldhagen's book is not a revision of everything that has been written on the Holocaust in the last fifty years. A solidly researched work on any of the topics Goldhagen touches—for instance, on the involvement of the Order Police in the Holocaust—would have been most welcome. As it stands, this book only caters to those who want simplistic answers to difficult questions, to those who seek the security of prejudices.

Why then review the book at such length? It was promoted aggressively in the mass media well before it was published and any historian had had a chance to read it. There is no limit to what a professional American marketing strategy can achieve, but to date, hardly any inroads into academia have been made by this book. Its marketing presents a challenge to the scholarly community. When the historical agenda can be dictated by advertising and marketing, professional historians must respond.

The discourse among scholars, as it has evolved over the centuries, respects certain rules: arguments count, not the people pushing them. One discusses the factual value of arguments and does not defame their authors. These rules are well worth defending. One can learn from a time when Einstein's theories, for example, were rejected, not because of the arguments themselves but because their proponent represented "Jewish physics." So far, all of the experts in the area of the Holocaust, regardless of their personal background, have been unanimous in severely criticizing Goldhagen's book. That this is the case, fifty years after the fact, and on such a highly emotional and complex subject, is a very hopeful sign.

$$\begin{array}{r} \overset{3}{9}.\overset{4}{5}\,8 \\ \underline{\,6} \\ 57.48 \end{array}$$